THE OTHER SIDE OF THE HILL

More Tug Hill Tales

Harold E. Samson

NORTH COUNTRY BOOKS
Box 86 — Lakemont, N.Y. 14857

First Printing — June, 1974

Second Printing — June, 1975

ISBN 978-1-4930-7671-0

PRINTED IN THE UNITED STATES OF AMERICA
BY BOONVILLE GRAPHICS, BOONVILLE, N. Y.

*This book dedicated to Alice,
my wife of many years.*

ACKNOWLEDGMENTS

The author wishes to hereby thank the following newspapers and publications for valuable background information and confirming facts found in their pages: The Watertown Daily Times; The Sandy Creek News; History of Lewis County, N. Y. 1880-1965; Evart's History of Oswego County; Jefferson County Centennial, 1905; Jefferson County Gazeteer; Memories of the Old Homestead; Five and Ten; Our Own Birds; Birds of America; Steele's Popular Zoology.

Also, thanks are hereby given to the following individuals for information, anecdotes, and the use of photographs reproduced herein: Carl Brenon, Charles Graves, Mrs. Ethel Higby, Mrs. Glenn Post, and Wallace Jackinski, all of Lowville; Mrs. Frank Bates, Clarence Johnson, Mrs. Perry Butts, and Elwin Rowell, Glenfield; Mr. and Mrs. Ernest Markham and Mrs. Emily Williams, Turin; Mrs. Laura Ferrance, Deer River; John Clemons (deceased), Osceola; Anthony Campany, Croghan; Homer Rebb, Burrville; Orrin Heath, Rodman; Eric Dutton, Adams; Richard Knobloch, Diamond; Mrs. Corrine Hasseler, Watertown; Rolla MacFarland, Depauville; and Ben Jones, Martinsburg.

Very special thanks to Miss Nanette Hamer, former Sandy Creek Town Historian, for the loan of notes, clippings, and general information.

INTRODUCTION

When *"Tug Hill Country"* made its appearance three years ago, I received many letters informing me that, although the readers enjoyed the book, they were mildly disappointed that it did not contain more stories from the eastern section of the Tug Hill Plateau, specifically around Lowville, Glenfield, Turin, et cetera.

The reason for this dereliction is obvious. It is much easier to research incidents that occurred near home than to go far afield for one's information, especially when only spare time is available for such work. But I felt that the good folks of the eastern sector should not be neglected, that they had as much right as anyone to have their stories told.

So, eastern readers, here is your book, "THE OTHER SIDE OF THE HILL." It is the answer to the many requests for another of the same format as *"Tug Hill Country,"* but with more attention paid to anecdotes with an eastern setting. In it I have tried to set down the day to day life as it was years ago in the area. Many people have been kind and patient enough to answer countless questions and relate stories on taped interviews, from which much of the manuscript was prepared. I have tried to be sure that everything told herein (with the exception of the tall tales) is as authentic as possible. I sincerely hope that you enjoy it.

Many people have asked me the origin of the name "Tug Hill." I am sorry not to be able to answer this with any degree of assurance, in spite of countless queries put to people whom I hoped might know the answer. Invariably, with those who professed to know, each answer was different from the ones before, and they have ranged from the ridiculous to the sublime.

Perhaps somewhere in the pot-pouri the truth lies buried, but if this is so, I have not been able to distinguish it. In the meantime, for want of a better explanation it might be well to heed the comment of one old-timer who informed me, "It used to be a tug-of-war sometimes just to make a livin' up there."

Many people have assisted in the preparation of this book by furnishing valued data, anecdotes, and information, as well as the loan of precious photographs for copying. To these goes my heartfelt thanks. Their names are listed in the acknowledgments, and if I have forgotten anyone I hereby humbly apologize.

I have tried to make this a factual and informative, and at the same time, an interesting book. If even a few readers judge it as such, I shall consider my efforts well spent.

TABLE OF CONTENTS

ILLUSTRATIONS

GROWING UP ON TUG HILL

As has been said time after time, life on Tug Hill was rough and hard, but extremely rewarding. And the same could be said of the process of growing up in that wild and beautiful region.

As was the case in most rural communities in those old days, infant mortality was very high as compared to present times. A rather large percentage of the babies born then were destined to decorate this vale of tears for only a few short years; then they succumbed to one or another of the childhood diseases and afflictions that have since been rendered by medical science either totally extinct, or only mildly annoying for a few days in case they occur at all.

Vaccinations and inoculations were either non-existent or only vaguely heard of, especially by back-country folks. Usually a child was expected to run the gamut of juvenile ailments; some of which, combatted by herbs and other home remedies, could and did lead to very serious results. Diphtheria, dysentery, scarlet and typhiod fevers, all claimed their full quotas of young victims. Today, these diseases are safeguarded against and rarely heard of, and if they occur at all, seldom have serious or lasting effects.

But once safely by the dangerous years, boys and girls who grew up on Tug Hill years ago inherited a legacy of health and ruggedness that usually lasted them throughout the remainder of their lives. Fresh, pure air, rough but nourishing food, hard work, and temperate living habits changed the boys into stalwart and broad-shouldered young men well suited to combat the rigorous living conditions ahead. And they brought the bloom of health and natural beauty to the cheeks of the girls; and the strength of physique and character to render them efficient helpmates for future husbands, and the mothers of a continuing succession of healthful progeny.

Very few young people who grew up on Tug Hill ever obtained a superfluity of education. High schools and colleges were, because of geographical conditions, remote and generally unattainable. Most students received only the rudimentary knowledge of the "Three R's" furnished by the few small country schools that existed throughout the region. But in spite of this, many went on to do very well for themselves in the business and professional world. Doctors, lawyers, judges, and many successful businessmen, as well as farmers, storekeepers, and lumberjacks, all knew humble beginnings among the rugged slopes and backwoods farms of Tug Hill.

A true representative of this group is a charming lady who now resides between Copenhagen and Deer River. Although advanced in years, she still retains a sparkling and youthful outlook that is extremely refreshing. Born Laura Hulbert, near East Martinsburg, she upon marriage became Laura Ferrence; and now a widow, still lives upon the farm operated for years by her husband and herself. Most of the land she now rents; but she retains enough to each year raise a voluminous crop of flowers. Some of these she sells, but most are grown to satisfy her love of natural and beautiful things.

The natural reserve of good health and amazing resistance built up by growing up in the great outdoors, coupled with an abiding faith in God, have enabled Mrs. Ferrence to withstand a series of very serious operations and still emerge with a wonderfully cheerful outlook on life, a sparkling sense of humor, and a memory that recalls Tug Hill life in the early years of this century with amazing clarity.

It was the author's very good fortune to be able to have a lengthy talk with Mrs. Ferrence, during which she recited the tales of a girlhood on Tug Hill which immediately follow.

*   *   *   *   *

My forefathers came down Black River with all their possessions on a raft, and took up some government land near what is now East Martinsburg before there was another white man in that part of the country.

My father was brought up by his grandfather, who was a cooper at East Martinsburg, and made all sorts of barrels, sap bucket, churns, and so on. One of Pa's earliest recollections was of sleeping in a big box of shavings, with a wolf-hide under him and a bearskin over him. That was the first bed that he remembered.

At the age of ten he left home and got himself a job driving a big white mule towing a canal-boat on the Black River Canal. From that day on he always made his own way. But life was hard, as the other drivers on the canal resented his youth, and many a night he had to hide out and sleep in the brush along the canal banks.

He used to tell about "sports" who came up from New York and along the canal, bringing with them game-roosters that they fought at various places. A man who owned a hotel at Beech's Bridge had a pit out behind his hotel where these fights used to take place. Of course, the practice was against the law, but most sheriffs and other lawmen were inclined to turn a deaf ear and a winking eye to any complaint that they might receive.

When he was still a small boy he made two trips on foot from East Martinsburg to Rome. The first trip he drove a flock of geese to market, and the second time a drove of hogs. He said the hogs were much harder to drive, as they had minds and wills of their own.

When my father was fourteen, the first train came through East Martinsburg on the New York Central,

3

and he helped cut many a cord of ten-inch wood for use in the locomotives. This wood was stacked along the tracks and was picked up when needed.

There was an Indian settlement right near where my father was brought up, and one of his best friends was a half-breed Indian boy named John Burro. His father was a chief, and his mother a white woman. My father used to tell of the many things he learned from John Burro when they were boys together. I only remember seeing him twice, and he was a grown man then, of course.

After we moved to the Hill, John Burro used to come to our place at night. He would stop in on his way back from wherever it was that they took the Indians to . . . I think it was Hogansburg . . . and knock on my folks' bedroom window, and he and Pa would talk in the night. I can remember hearing him many times.

One time soon after we moved to the Hill, Pa started out for the barn in the morning, and on top of the two steps leading from our kitchen down into the woodshed he found a flour sack with a hind quarter of fresh-killed venison inside. Pa brought it in and put it on the table.

"John was here last night," he said. "I do wish he had stopped and had a talk with me."

When I first went up on Tug Hill to live, I was seven years old. My father had a little farm of thirty-two acres near Martinsburg, but it was not large enough to support a family of seven. So he bought a three hundred and fifty acre farm on the Houseville Gulf road up on the Hill; no money down and so much a year, and we moved in.

Our furniture was good enough, but nothing special. We had good beds, a good cook-stove, and so forth. We also had about a dozen head of cattle, a good team of horses, and a couple hundred sheep. We used to raise beautiful hogs, the long-snooted kind, and also fruit, grain, and potatoes. My father sold logs and timbers, and cordwood at two dollars and fifty cents a cord, delivered

4

to Lowville or Glenfield. My mother made excellent butter which was sold to the lumber camps higher up on the Hill; and the stores in Lowville always paid her two cents over the regular price.

In those days it was against the law to sell bob-veal (derived from butchering new-born calves) so we and the neighbors used to keep the calves we didn't care to raise for about six weeks and fatten them. Then my father would deliver ours and the neighbor's calves to Port Leyden, from where they were shipped to city markets.

Oh, we did anything and everything to make an honest living in those days. And people could do it today, if they tried. The land up there is just as good as it ever was, but most people don't have the backbone to work it and make it pay.

Every member of our family had his or her work to do, and we couldn't be lazy, as the welfare of the family depended on each one doing his part. I never liked housework, so I worked outdoors with my father. He used to call me his right-hand man.

People have too much nowadays. We didn't have much of the material things, but we had a wealth of the spiritual things, and we were very, very happy. On Sunday afternoons in summer we were content to walk around the farm, looking over the crops and the young stock; resting and enjoying ourselves.

And those winter evenings! After supper Pa would go down cellar and bring up a butter-bowl of big, pound-sweet apples. Then, while my mother sat and knitted, he would get down on our rag carpet and play dominoes and eat apples with us children. And when it was time for bed, he would sit on our couch with one of my brothers on each side of him, while I always got his lap, and finally he would bundle us up and take us to bed. And I can also remember how that mustache would tickle my ear when he kissed me goodnight. Oh, those memories! I

5

wouldn't give them up for all that I have or ever hope to have.

My father was a big handsome man, with black curly hair, and he always wore a mustache. He grew his first mustache at fourteen, so that he would look older and could hire out for more money. He chewed tobacco but never drank. He used to take us children out in the woods and teach us all about nature, much of which he had learned from John Burro. He told us what berries we could and could not eat, and how to build a fire in the woods, and what animals we should steer clear of, and that if we became lost, not to panic, but to find a stream and follow it downstream, and we would always come out somewhere.

He was no hand to go to church, but was a firm believer in God and always maintained that he didn't need a church to worship in his own way. He would go out each bright morning and face the sun, and maybe say a prayer to it. And he never ate a meal that he didn't thank God for what we had.

He loved the elements, and whenever possible he would stand and watch a thunder-storm gather. I remember once when I was helping him set up buckwheat, a big storm was making up in the west, and he stood there with a sheaf of buckwheat clasped to his breast and just watched that storm come up; and his face was just a-shining. Oh, if only I could have had that picture.

We had a little black bull that had a habit of running away and ending up at some of the neighbors miles away, so we got to calling him Johnny Runaway. It was always my job to go and fetch him home, but that wasn't so bad because I had trained him to ride bareback, and steer with a hackamore halter. He would usually be at either Delbert Sharms' place, or over at Flathammer's, which meant a round trip of a couple of hours, over a big hogs-

6

back and through a culvert under the Glenfield and Western Railroad.

One night I was bringing him home, following cow-paths through the woods. A big full moon was shining, and it was about as light as day; but I was in a hurry to get home, so I was urging him along with a little switch that I had broken off. We had just come to a little spring creek when Johnny Runaway suddenly decided that he wanted a drink. So he just put on his brakes, and I, taken unawares, just sailed right over his head and landed in a pool of water up to my neck.

To make matters all the worse, the son-of-a-gun ran away from me and I had to find my way through a pitchy-black grove of hemlocks and finally round him up and drive him the rest of the way home. Believe me, I'll never forget that experience.

My father's horses were always well cared for. They received four quarts of corn and oats three times a day, and only the best hay went into their mangers. No clover ever went into horse hay, only timothy and alfalfa.

I always was a great lover of horses, and as I grew up with them I came to know them pretty well — how to judge their characters and so forth. We had one colt that came from up Malone way that could speak only French; I mean he could only understand French. He grew to be a real big fellow, but when Pa came to break him to harness, he said the horse was balky.

Since he had practically grown up with me, I knew that he didn't have a balky bone in his body, but that something else was causing the trouble. I noticed that when he started to draw, he would always throw up his head before balking, so I figured that his collar was choking him, and told my father so. Pa put a larger collar on him, and that ended the trouble, once and for all.

Another time I believe I saved my dad's life from a horse that was really mean. Pa used to sometimes go out

7

in the spring and buy a "junk horse" for twelve or fourteen dollars; one that had something the matter with it like the heaves or spavins. He would doctor it up and use it on the farm for the summer, and then sell it in the fall for twenty or twenty-five dollars. This one mare he got was really vicious. She would bite or kick you every chance she got.

One day I was about to go into the barn when I heard dad scream, so I hurried in to see what was the matter. This mare had him trapped against the side of the stall, which was too high for him to climb over. She was curled around him like a rainbow, trying to reach him with either her teeth or her feet. Pa saw me coming and yelled for me to stay back.

"She'll take an arm off you If you get near," he shouted.

Well, I was only ten years old, but I figured an arm was only an arm, and it was my father that was in danger. And I was real quick in those days, so when she turned her head to bite at Pa, I reached in and unsnapped the halter rope. Then I picked up a beech club that was within reach and clouted her right between the ears. She forgot all about Pa and went out of that stall like the Devil was after her. She never went back in a stall again as long as we had her, which was not very long.

Sometimes you found yourself in danger, but it was all in the day's work.

The first milk station ever built in the area was at East Martinsburg, and was called McDermitt Station. There was a big ice-house there that the farmers used to fill in the winter so that there would be ice for packing the milk cars in the summer. No refrigerated cars then, except by the use of this ice. The farmers delivered the milk there twice a day, and the "Flying Milk" would come through and pick up those cars.

East Martinsburg as I knew it then was a busy place.

8

Besides the milk station, there were two cheese factories, a store, a schoolhouse that took care of about seventy-five scholars, a freight yard, a big sawmill with boarding house and company houses, a cider mill, a grist mill, and quite a few houses. And lumber — the place was lumber from one end to the other. A lot of this was brought down from sawmills up on Tug Hill to be shipped on the railroad.

Like most of the other farmers in the area, my father did a lot of this lumber hauling in the winter when times were slack. He had a beautiful team that was known far and wide as "Hulbert's Bays," and he really knew how to work them and take care of them. At the end of a day's work he rubbed them down and washed their legs with Castile soap; and when he had to spend the night away from home, instead of going to bed he took his 45-70 rifle and a blanket and slept in the manger to protect his team. There were many gangs stealing horses in those days, and a mans' team was often his livelihood.

One of these gangs of horse-thieves was known as The Loomis Gang, and they really made a name for themselves. They traveled far and wide stealing horses, and anything else that wasn't nailed down. They would take the horses to hideouts that they had around and completely change their appearances before putting them up for sale. They knew how to change or add markings, such as bleaching hair to make stars in foreheads that had been plain before, or adding white stockings to dark colored legs, or taking away markings by the use of dye. Some of these changes were so good that men were known to have bought horses that had been stolen from them earlier, and never knew the difference until later.

What is now known as Tabolt's Corners used to be Gulfhead, and was a station on the Glenfield and Western Railroad. There was a cheese factory there, and across a little swale from this was a big farm with a big,

9

square-roofed white house that belonged to Mr. Tabolt. I guess the place had belonged in the Tabolt family for a couple of generations. Georgia-Pacific, which now owns all this land until recently held by the Gould Paper Company, has a gate across the old Glenfield and Western railroad bed, now used as a truck road, at this point.

Page was a sawmill town about five or six miles farther along this railroad, and was founded by Page and Fairchild, a lumbering firm from Oswego, N. Y., who also built the railroad. Page was also known as No. 22, and was the second settlement to bear that name. The first was five miles to the south, and later became known as Michigan Mills. My father hauled the big boilers for the mill up into Page with our old horses, Chris and Maude. Lon Campbell had a big sawmill there, also a boarding house. There was a man by the name of Loomis who ran the store and hotel, and had a big hotel barn. There was a big spring there and, my, was that water good. Those old boilers that my father hauled up in there are all that is left of Page.

Many interesting tales are told about Page, and one of them concerns an incident that my father knew to be true, because he was there and saw it.

There was a fellow came through there with a dancing and wrestling bear, and he put up at the hotel for the night. During the evening the teamsters and lumberjacks there had a lot of fun with the bear, and as he loved beer, they fed him a lot of it. Along about midnight the man took his bear to the barn for the night, and he slept there with him.

The next morning the barn door was open and the bear was gone. So was the trainer, all except what was inside his boots, which lay there on the floor. They figured that it must have been the excessive amount of beer that the animal had drunk that caused him to go

10

berserk and kill and eat his trainer. No one ever saw the bear again.

Annie Rinkenberg ran a big boarding house near Page, and Mike Dunn and "One-eyed Cushman" used to have big farms near there. Everything is all grown up there now.

We used to see and hear lots of wild animals in those old days, many of which were considered dangerous. But somehow, I was never very afraid of wild animals. I used to fish all those streams around there, usually alone except for my two dogs that went with me on these trips. I knew nothing could touch me while they were around.

I have seen wolves, and panthers were not uncommon. We used to hear them all the time as they used to travel up across our woods when they were on their travels, especially in September and October. My father told me to keep out of the woods when they were around, but I was a girl who was all doubt, and wanted to see for myself.

Well, I got my chance one time. It was on the Morgan Gulf road as you are coming up from Houseville. You know where you come up that first big hill, and then you come up that winding hill? It was on that winding hill that I first came into contact with a panther.

I was fourteen at the time, going on fifteen, and I had taken a big load of potatoes into Lowville, and was coming back with a big load of feed. It was getting along toward dark when I came up that big hill, and at the top there's a sort of hogsback that runs in toward Whetstone Gulf. When I was right up there is when I first heard that panther scream.

Now, I usually walked up that hill when I was pulling a load, to make it easier on the horses, but I didn't walk it that night. The horses were scared, and so was I. I got down on my knees and got the board across the

11

front of the wagon box up against my chest, and hung onto those lines for dear life.

Of couse I knew where the biggest stones were in the road, having traveled it so much. I said to myself, "If I can keep the wheels in the tracks, and the harness holds and the neap don't break, we'll make it alright." Well, God was with me and we made it, but believe me, we really traveled.

The panther came right up alongside the road, and every now and then he'd let a yowl out of him, and the horses really traveled. I kept the wheels right in the tracks so they wouldn't hit the big stones, and we covered that last mile home in pretty fast time.

When we pulled into the yard, my father came out and said, "Seems to me you're pushing them horses plenty hard," and I said, "Believe me, I didn't have to push them," and then I told him what had happened.

Well, the next morning about half an inch of snow had fallen, it being late October, and I started out to see if I could find the panther's track. I slipped a tea-saucer in my frock pocket and took off down there, 'cause I could really run in those days. I found where he had crossed the road, and that tea-saucer just covered his track in the snow. He sure was a big one, I can tell you.

Another time, my brother Harry, who was two years older than I, and I went fishing in the beautiful little spring creek that flowed across the road near our house. My father had made us some new birch fish-poles that we were anxious to try out. We were sneaking up on a good trout-hole when we heard a noise down beneath a big rock that overhung the water. We jumped up on the rock and looked down, and there was a big, gray animal fishing. It looked up and saw us, and started to climb out, and we started for home.

I had heard my mother tell that if you keep facing an animal it will never charge you, so we went toward

12

home back-to-back; me facing the animal and Harry picking the way. It followed along behind us, probably more out of curiosity than anything else, but we didn't know that; and it kept on following right into our pasture lot, where we made for home in a hurry. When we told Pa what had happened he told us not to be scared, that it was probably just a big coon.

He called my older brother Earl, and Earl started to take down the shotgun, but Pa winked at Earl and said, "No, take the 45-70." When I heard that I knew it was no coon, but I had known that anyway, as I had seen pictures of Canadian lynx with their tufted ears, and I knew that's what it was.

Earl said when they got back that the lynx had followed us right up close to our place, and then had climbed a tree and that was the last sign they could find of him. We small kids weren't allowed to go after the cows for a few days after that.

Now, after you went past where my folks lived, the next place was the old Phillips place, and then the Charlie Stein place, and then the Mel Ames place. Just between there and the Corrigan Hill road there used to be a culvert that had quite a story connected with it. There used to be a stagecoach line through there . . . went to Watertown, I guess.

Well, somebody robbed a stage-coach right there by that culvert and got quite a cache of money and jewelry. For some reason they didn't dare take it away, so they buried it right there. They also killed a negro and buried him with it to protect it, so the story goes. I don't know this to be so, but they used to tell that if anyone went there to dig for the treasure, the thunder would roll and the lightning would flash. If they kept right on that negro would come out and parade up and down the road.

One time my brother Earl was home, and a couple

13

fellows he knew were there too. One of them said, "Let's go down there and dig, just for fun." So about nine o'clock they took shovels and started out. What happened, I don't know. They got home about midnight, and from that time on, no one could ever get any of them to talk about the incident again. Whatever they saw or heard they didn't tell.

My mother used to tell me to keep away from the place. I wasn't exactly afraid, but when I was coming by there I'd walk on the other side of the road, and hustle a little.

Now between this place and the Whetstone Gulf is what they call the narrows, and this is where the big caves are. The fellow who shot Minnie Ingersol over on the Flat Rock Road got away from the law and hid out in these caves for three or four months. His sister lived right near there, and used to smuggle food in to him. Finally she talked him into coming out and giving himself up to the law. I used to hear that he ended up in the electric chair.

There was an incident that occurred in LaBree's lumber camp up on the Hill years ago that I have heard them tell about. A fellow who was a professional cardshark, but who must also have been possessed by the Devil to a certain degree, came into the camp to stay over night, and after supper when the men were all gathered in the lobby, he showed them some tricks. He tossed a deck of cards up to the ceiling and they stuck right there. Then he would make bets with the men that he could call down any card that he wanted, and he would always do it, without fail. Later, he had them stoke up the lobby stove until it was nearly red hot, and he offered to bet that he could let down his britches and set his bare rear-end on that stove without getting burned. Of course he got plenty of bets on that, and he did just as he had said without seeming to feel the heat at all.

14

Certainly, the Devil must have been looking out for his own that night.

Another man who used to live at Beech's Bridge was also possessed by the Devil, my father always said. He maintained that without the Devil's help he couldn't do some of the things that he did. When he met the fellow on the road, Pa always managed to keep the width of the dirt road between them. Somehow, he believed that the stretch of raw dirt would protect him from the influence of the Devil.

Not that the fellow had a sinister or dangerous appearance. He always drove a span of beautiful bay horses, and always appeared friendly enough. In fact, he was always laughing. On a clear day you could hear him coming a mile away, laughing away to himself like crazy.

Once, when they were putting the road through from Lowville to Beech's Bridge, the men were trying to move a big boulder out of the right-of-way. My father was working there with his team, and they had several teams hooked to the rock, trying to drag it out of the way, but they couldn't budge it.

Well, along comes this man, as usual laughing for all he was worth. He says, "Unhitch your horses, boys, and let me move it for you." Of course they thought he was trying to show off, but they unhitched as he had said; and he put his back up against that rock, dug his heels into the dirt, gave a big heave, and pushed that boulder right out into Black River. And there it is to this day, or at least it was until they built the new bridge a few years ago. Now no man could do a thing like that without some kind of unearthly help.

In later life I married the son of a family by the name of Ferrance, who lived on the road from Gulfhead to Highmarket, which is just about the highest point on the Hill. When the notice came through for my husband to register for the draft in World War I, he was working for

15

the McCarthy brothers away up on the Hill, shoveling skidways and loading logs. I knew he had to get that notice, so I put on my snowshoes and hiked up through where the "new road" ran, and sent word to him by Frankie Bates, conductor on the Glenfield and Western Railroad. It was fifty degrees below zero that night, and I had to stop at the Tabolt place on the way back, to get warm. My husband walked out home that night, and the next day, when we went to Turin for him to registser, it was still fifty below.

*　*　*　*　*

It was such things as these that made the old-time residents of Tug Hill the tough, independent, self-sufficient breed that they were. All too few of them are left.

THE ORIGIN OF
THE IROQUOIS

If one is to believe an old Indian legend, the very beginning of the tribe that later developed into the powerful Iroquois Nation, took place on the northwest flank of Tug Hill. It was supposed to have occurred on the banks of a small stream that ran northward into the South Branch of Sandy Creek. This would place the site somewhere in the Allendale-Lorraine area, a section noted for its precipitous gulfs and wierd rock formations.

According to the myth, the Great Spirit one day sent down a blinding lightning bolt that opened a great rift in the rocky cliffs along the stream; and out of this rift walked hand in hand a red-skinned man and woman. Making their way downstream, the couple soon came to the larger stream, and there they built a hut, "where the salmon crowded the rapid in floodtime, where the beaver abounded, and where the forests were filled with deer and moose."

Here in this hunters' paradise they lived and reared their family, and thus became the very nucleus of the famed Iroquois Nation. At first these people were of a very peaceful nature, content to till the soil and grow their corn, beans, and other vegetables. The streams gave them a bountiful supply of fish, and the forests yielded an unending source of game. Life was serene and beautiful.

But as time went by and their numbers increased, they naturally began to spread out into otherwise unclaimed territories. This process probably took up several centuries in time, at least many generations. When their wanderings had led them as far north as the great river of St. Lawrence, their infiltration began to encroach on lands claimed by the fierce and warlike Ottawas, a tribe versed in the skills of battle and the chase. Of course the intruders from the south were no match for these people in wilderness warfare, and were quickly conquered and made a subservient tribe.

The cruelty and tyranny of the Ottawas at last forced the Iroquois into open rebellion, and thus began an attack-and-retreat warfare that lasted for several years. In these encounters the Iroquois were usually bested because of their inferior knowledge of fighting tactics. But what they lacked in fighting skill, they made up for in bravery and tenacity, and each newly contested hunting ground or village was fiercely defended. This may account to some extent for the many remains of settlements and crude fortifications that have been found throughout northern New York.

At last despairing of ever winning the interminable succession of skirmishes, or of ever being left to live in peace, the Iroquois, according to legend, finally retreated to the south and east, into what is now central New York State, and here they decided to make their permanent home. Their years of struggle with the Ottawas had at least been to their advantage in one respect; they had gained greatly in their knowledge of warfare from their constant contention with the northern tribes. So warlike had they become, in fact, that the other tribes native to this new territory along the Mohawk River and the Finger Lakes quickly decided that it would be very much to their advantage to form a peaceful alliance with the newcomers.

And so it was that the powerful five nations of the Iroquois came into being. Over countless council fires their separate people were welded into an organization of

18

unprecedented power and wisdom; against which all neighboring tribes found it futile to contend. Soon their warlike tendencies, their strength and wisdom, had made them the undisputed masters of all New York State, as well as northern Pennsylvania.

The name "Iroquois" was adopted as the official designation for the Five Nations. According to the old legend, the word meant, literally, "they who smoke," or "people who smoke," and may have been suggested by the countless peace pipes consumed around the many council fires. History has proven the gigantic stature that the name assumed in the development of the state.

Now this is just one legend concerning the origin of the Iroquois people. The author knows that there are many more such, but this is the one he prefers to believe; that one of the most powerful and warlike tribes in the history of the entire nation began right here in the Lesser Wilderness, in the very loins of ancient Tug Hill.

OLD "GEE WHIZ,"
THE GLENFIELD AND
WESTERN RAILROAD

Of the hundreds of lumberjacks, sawmill men, and bark peelers who helped to harvest the millions of feet of pulp and hardwood that came down from the forests of Tug Hill between the turn of the century and three decades later, nearly every one was familiar with the old "Gee Whiz." For this was the sentimental nickname of the Glenfield and Western Railroad that began at Glenfield and ran for almost thirty-five circuitous miles up over the ridges, swamps, and streams of eastern Tug Hill to a point in Campbell Wood, in the town of Montague.

To say that nearly every one of these men was familiar with the Glenfield and Western is no exaggeration, for this was primarily a lumbering railroad and any other purpose for which it was used was purely coincidental. There was practically no one on Tug Hill or in the surrounding area who had not either helped to build and maintain it, or cut logs for it to transport. In its heyday it exerted a powerful influence on the economy of the region, and for over a quarter of a century it contributed much to the welfare of the families which lived near it. Folks grew from childhood to adulthood with the sound of the labored chug-chug and the mournful wail of its two locomotives in their ears. And when it was finally gone, it left a void in the lives of many that will never be filled.

The first actual work on the route of the line was

21

done, ironically, long before its start or even its inception. In the winter of 1853 a fifteen-hundred-foot-long cut was blasted and dug through an extensive ledge of rock between Glenfield and Houseville by the Ogdensburg, Clayton and Rome Railroad Co. This rockcut was twenty feet wide and twenty feet deep, and was built to accommodate a railroad that they intended to construct through the territory. But unfortunately for this enterprise, the Rome, Watertown and Ogdensburg Railroad Company was busy at the same time projecting a parallel route a few miles farther west, with the same general goal, the shipping business of the North Country, as an objective.

The route selected by this line possessed much more gentle grades than that of the Ogdensburg, Clayton and Rome Co.; passing as it did through the lowlands along the western base of Tug Hill. In addition, this company believed in laying rails as soon as the grading of each section was completed, and this enabled them to utilize the sections of track already built in the progress of the work ahead. On the other hand, the Ogdensburg, Clayton, and Rome outfit believed in fully completing the grading before the laying of track began.

The end result of the competiiton was that the Rome, Watertown, and Ogdensburg reached completion before much trackage had been laid by the opposing line, which gave up in defeat, knowing that it would be much too late to capture an equitable portion of the available business.

When the Glenfield and Western was built some forty-eight years later, this abandoned rock-cut proved to be a valuable asset in getting from lower ground to higher and vice versa, so it was utilized. However, it proved to be a vulnerable target for deep-drifting Tug Hill snows; and in spite of the eleven hundred and ninety feet of six-foot-high snow fence built to protect it, many times it drifted full and required several days to clear its length.

The need for a railroad from the heights of Tug Hill to join the Utica and Black River Division of the New York Central began to be felt late in the last century. About 1887, a group of business men from Michigan built a large sawmill in the western section of the Town of Highmarket, which was named Michigan Mills after its owners. The product of this mill was transported to Port Leyden by teams and wagons, or sleighs, but the grueling eighteen-mile haul proved to be very costly and cut deeply into the profits of the enterprise. After a disastrous fire in Port Leyden, which destroyed a newly-constructed veneer finishing plant, the company sold their forest holdings to a man by the name of Pond, also from Michigan.

In May of 1892, Mr. Pond in turn sold his timberlands to Page, Fairchild and Co. of Oswego, N. Y. Thereupon the name of Michigan Mills was changed to Page. Later, another mill was built by the company about five miles northeast of Page, and the little hamlet that grew up around it was designated as Number Twenty-Two, as it stood on lot No. 22.

Page and Fairchild believed that a cheaper mode of transportation for the product of their two mills could be devised. Accordingly, a wooden tram road was constructed between the two mills, and continued for two miles farther north to a terminus in the Town of Martinsburg. This terminus was known as Number Six because it was built on lot No. 6. Most of this route was downhill, which provided much easier and faster transportation. However, at Number Six the lumber had to be reloaded onto wagons or sleighs, and drawn down through Martinsburg, mostly by the Corrigan Hill road, to East Martinsburg, where it was loaded into railroad

23

cars for shipment. This reduced the overall hauling distance by some six miles.

However, this necessitated an extra handling of the material, and was still an expensive system, so still other methods were pondered upon. It became increasingly evident that a railroad over Tug Hill was sorely needed. So in 1900 the Glenfield and Western Railroad Company was incorporated, with capital stock of $295,000. The principal stockholders were Allison Page, P. A. Page, Woodby Page, and David Fairchild, all of Oswego; M. S. Weldon of Carthage; and C. E. Campbell of New York City. The stupendous job of laying out the route of the proposed line over the forbidding hump of Tug Hill was entrusted to G. C. Lawrence, C. E. Brownell, and J. P. Brownell, all of Carthage.

Once the railroad was definitely decided upon, its protagonists were not slow in implementing its beginning. Supervision of the actual construction fell to E. D. Bennett, of Pulaski, and the first grading was done at Glenfield early in 1901. Under the superintendency of J. M. Humes, the work went along well, and by August 6, 1902, track had been completed to Houseville and traffic was opened to that point. And then on December 1, 1902, Page and Fairchild sold all their holdings, including not only the woodlands but also the railroad with its trackage, rolling stock, and buildings, to the Gould Paper Company of Lyons Falls.

In 1901, Page and Fairchild had moved their mill at Page to the new site at No. 22, where it was combined with the mill already there. At this time No. 22 assumed the name of Page, and the first Page, now virtually a ghost-town, reverted to Michigan Mills.

For almost twelve years Page had a post-office. This was established September 18, 1900, with George Loomis as postmaster, and was housed in Mr. Loomis' store building. When the move to No. 22 was made, the postoffice went along also, where it continued to be used until January 31, 1912. It is not recorded that Page ever had but one postmaster.

When the Gould Paper Company took over the Glenfield and Western, the total track already built was 19.55 miles. This distance embraced over one hundred curves, some of them very sharp. In fact, less than half of the track was straight. The steepest grade was said to have been two hundred and seventy-seven feet of rise to the mile, or a little over five per cent. The official railroad inspection report for 1903 listed it as the steepest line with the most curves and bridges of any in New York State.

When complete, it crossed thirty bridges, thirteen cattle passes, forty-three culverts, and had fifteen retaining and diversion walls. It also had twenty-three miles of barbed wire fence and eleven hundred and ninety feet of six-foot-high snow fence.

The rails were of comparatively light weight, being only sixty pounds to the yard, and were laid upon ties spaced twenty-six hundred to the mile. The first telephone line to serve the railroad was built in 1902, and had but one wire attached to poles spaced thirty-five to the mile.

At first the line boasted only one locomotive, but a good one for the type of terrain it had to master. This was No. 22, a Shay engine geared for double power for use in mountainous country. By no stretch of the imagination could she have been termed a speed merchant, as her top capacity was about fifteen miles per hour. But her reliability more than made up for her lack of speed, and she served the line faithfully and well throughout its duration.

Later another locomotive, No. 75, was especially built for the line by the American Locomotive Company. No. 75 was an eight-wheeler and geared for more

25

speed than No. 22. She carried four thousand gallons of water and nine tons of fuel. This engine outlived the line, and was later bought by another northern line, where she continues to give service.

In addition to the engines, the line boasted six flat-cars, three Sheffield motor cars, and three push cars. A model-T Ford car was converted by some of the company's mechanical geniuses to run upon the rails, and was called the "Jitney." This speedy little contraption was used for the transportation of railroad officials and personnel, and for passengers who were in a hurry and didn't mind open-air discomforts.

The right-of-way was three rods wide and was mowed each year with hand scythes, except for the strip between the rails. This was kept clear of weeds by a mowing machine pushed ahead of a motor car. In 1922 another weed eradicator was introduced, this being a flail-type something along the line of the modern "chicken-pickers" now used by highway crews. According to tales of the workers who ran this machine, it did a wonderful job of kicking up a cloud of dust, but did very little damage to the weeds.

Of course, the line also possessed another very essential piece of equipment, a snowplow. To cope with Tug Hill snow it had to be very ruggedly built. Its overall length was thirty-five feet and the width was ten feet, with two side wings attached. It weighed fifty-two thousand pounds, a right hefty load to push up some of those grades. This plow once broke loose from the engine in Morgan Gulf, one of the steepest grades on the line. Apparently there didn't happen to be much snow on the tracks that day, as the plow took off like a scared rabbit. The engine crew chased it but could not catch up with it, so they stopped at the Houseville depot and phoned ahead to Glenfield, warning them to be on the lookout for it. They were somewhat surprised when from the other end of the wire came the answer,

"Look out for it, hell. It just got here."

At Glenfield, the fast-traveling plow had jumped the track and hit the engine house, doing considerable damage. A workman, Warren Johnson, was hurt in the accident. He was never able to work after that, and died soon after.

Quite a few buildings were built by the Glenfield and Western in the early years. In 1901 a freight house and coal shed were built in Glenfield, each of those structures being sixteen feet by thirty-six feet. Coal was shoveled from flat-bottomed coal cars brought in on the New York Central line into the coal shed, and was then shoveled out again into the tenders of the two locomotives. Also in Glenfield, a so-called roundhouse was built the same year. This structure, thirty-two feet by sixty-five feet, was a roundhouse in name only, as it had no turntable, and was used for storage and repair work only. Actually, the engines were turned around on a "Y." The year 1901 also saw the construction of a sand storehouse, twenty by twenty-four feet. In 1902, a water tank twelve feet in diameter and ten feet high was built of cypress at the Glenfield terminal.

About this time, probably in 1901, several tar-paper-covered shacks were built for the use of laborers on the line. These were twelve by sixteen feet in size, and though not prepossessing on the outside, were quite comfortable. Also built at Page was a twenty by sixty foot warehouse and coal shed, with an attached water tank. Water for this tank was furnished by a dam across a small stream, and was forced into the tank by a hydraulic ram.

The depot in Houseville was built in 1901, and was twenty-four by seventy-three feet in dimension. The railroad used only one of the five downstairs rooms, the remaining ones being rented to Emery Jones, and later M.

27

W. Solomon, for a feed store. Of course, Houseville, originally named for Ebenezer House, had been in possession of a postoffice since 1828. Now, with a railroad running through the hamlet, it bid fair to become a thriving little community; but the extra growth did not materialize and the post office was discontinued on December 15, 1911.

In 1907, a twelve by thirty-two foot coal bin was built at Glenfield, and a tool house measuring twelve by sixteen feet. It was not until eighteen years later, in 1925, that the railroad-tie treating plant was established there. This contained a vertical boiler twenty-four by seventy-two feet, and a vat twenty-seven by twenty-eight by ten feet. The boiler was used only to heat the creosote solution in which the ties were immersed. There was no pressure treating as in some of the more sophisticated treating plants.

The water tower at Fish Creek, at one time the western terminus of the line, was a Fairbanks Morse cedar tank of ten thousand gallons capacity. It was filled from Fish Creek by a Rife hydraulic ram.

In 1907 the railroad was extended from Fish Creek to Monteola, a little logging hamlet named for the two townships, Montague and Osceola, upon whose boundaries it stood.

As has been stated, there were many small bridges, culverts and cattle passes on the line. Starting at Glenfield and proceeding generally west up over the Hill, some of the cattle passes mentioned were at the farms of Lem Goodrich, Jason Mumford, Arthur Goodwin, Cliff Lee, Ray Meiss, and Howard Phelps. Another at the Bardo farm accommodated both cattle and a small stream. Two bridges spanned the rock cut on the Houseville-Glenfield road, with others at Whetstone Creek, Houseville Creek, Fish Creek, and Six-Mile Creek.

At the head of Morgan Gulf, where the line finally

climbed out onto fairly level ground for a few miles, there was a small waiting shack known as Gulfhead Station, now Tabolts Corners. Here were also located a cheese factory and a large farm with a big white farmhouse owned by a Mr. Tabolt.

About two and a half miles west of here, a pontoon bridge carried the tracks over a marshy, flooded section. This pontoon affair proved to be very unsatisfactory because of its unstable, up and down action when a train passed over. So the pontoons were sunk and stones piled on top, over which were placed timbers that carried the ties, and in turn the rails. This arrangement soon solidified into a compact and substantial causway, that today carries a truck road over the flooded area.

There were many wrecks and derailments, mostly of a minor nature. The main line was graded for track, but the many spur tracks that ran out into the woods were laid along ungraded stream beds. This fact caused quite a bit of trouble because of derailments at switches.

There was only one wreck during the life of the line that could be blamed directly for a fatality. This occurred near Bardo's crossing on October 23, 1917, when two carloads of logs and the caboose carrying passengers were derailed. The caboose was crushed by the tumbling logs, killing Edward Darling, a passenger, and injuring Marvin King and Harmon Swan.

Another time Number Twenty-Two couldn't make up her mind which of the two tracks to follow at a switch. The front wheels chose one and the hind wheels the other, with the result that Twenty-two ended up crosswise of the track with her front end overhanging a swampy stream. This happened at one of the spongy switches already mentioned.

When Seventy-five decided to pull her caper, she certainly came up with a dandy. Leaving the track she plowed off into the right-of-way and ended up half buried in the muck and ooze of a trackside swamp. Moreover, she was tilted at a precarious angle of almost forty-five degrees, which did not help any in the ticklish job of getting her back on the track.

The line did not own a crane larger than a log loader, which was quite incapable of lifting a locomotive of Seventy-five's stature, so the job had to be accomplished by jacking and blocking. It took two full weeks to replace the forty-eight-foot engine back on the tracks where she belonged. It is safe to assume that traffic was badly hampered during that period.

At Gulfhead, loaded log trains were stopped and the brakes on all the cars were set up hard and fast by the use of pickaxe handles in the brake wheels. This was for the trip down Morgan Gulf, which contained many sharp curves and a formidable grade. It is said that the grinding, spark-throwing trip down the Gulf often resulted in flat spots on the wheels.

Interspersed with all the labor, trouble, and responsibility of operating this cantankerous railroad were incidents of comedy and humor that the few remaining erstwhile employees like to remember. One of these concerned Leslie Johnson, a later superintendent of the line, who took over that position around 1920. Mr. Johnson had a brother, Mord, who worked for the line as a brakeman and general handyman.

Leslie, the super, was a total abstainer from strong drink, and would not tolerate its use by his employees while on duty. On the other hand, brother Mord went to just the other extreme. Somewhere along the line he had a friend who made a practice of dispensing Tug Hill moonshine, and Mord was one of his best customers. It became a habit of his to stop whichever train he was on while he patronized this friend, and in due time Leslie became aware of this fact.

It does not seem plausible that he could have done

other than to warn his brother at least once, maybe several times, of the possible consequences of his actions. If so, the warnings must have gone unheeded, and Leslie must have gotten fed up. Anyway, one day when Mord's train was late, Leslie fired his brother forthwith. He also made it plain that Mord would not be rehired, and Mord left the area, never to return.

Now this incident might not have seemed funny to Mord, but it tickled the funnybones of most of his fellow employees, and established Leslie's reputation for fair play and non-favoritism.

Another time, a certain train crew watched a flock of young turkeys all summer while they grew up on a farm that bordered the tracks. Among themselves they planned to each have one of those birds when they were grown up and the proper time arrived.

One night when they figured the time was propitious, six of them walked quietly down along the tracks to carry out their raid. Everything went well until each man had secured a bird and they were ready to leave, when somehow or other one man got locked in the turkey house. Of course he was terrified of being left behind, and began to shout,

"Get me outa here. Get me outa here."

In fact, he shouted so loud that he woke up the farmer, who got up and started to investigate, but suddenly changed his mind and went back to bed, probably grinning to himself. The man locked in the turkey house had a speech deficiency which forced him to talk through his nose. His voice was easily recognizable, and quickly identified him to the farmer, who thereby had a pretty shrewd idea who the other culprits were from having seen the whole crew many times.

The next morning after delivering his milk to Glenfield, the farmer drove over to the roundhouse where the train crew was preparing to go out on a run. Confronting

31

them with the fact that he knew who had raided his turkey house the night before and carried away six birds, he informed them that unless pay for the fowl was forthcoming, he had it in his mind to have a talk with the sheriff.

Seeing that denial would be of no use, the culprits admitted their guilt and proceeded to cough up the pay for the purloined birds. And it can safely be supposed that the price demanded was for strictly first class merchandise.

In 1918, the Dexter Sulphite Pulp and Paper Company, having cut off most of the softwood in their holdings, decided to make use of the hardwood. Selecting Glenfield as a site, they built there a sawmill that was reputed to be the largest one in the world at that time. This was really two mills side by side, each equipped with a large band-saw, resaw, edger, slasher, trimmer, etc.; in short, each a complete mill in itself. The logs were dumped into a hotpond where they were thoroughly washed, after which they were drawn up into the center of the combined mills on an endless chain. Here they could be placed on the rollway of either mill by a hydraulic kicker that could operate either right or left.

This was called the Monteola Hardwood Mill. It ran full time during the spring, summer and fall, but when the deep snows of winter came it was very hard to keep a sufficient supply of logs on hand. Its very size defeated its own purpose. The Glenfield and Western continued to do its best to supply the voracious appetite of this giant, but the adverse winter weather of the Hill ruled against this. So in 1927 Dexter Sulphite sold its mill and its interest in the Glenfield and Western to the Keystone Wood, Chemical and Lumber Company of Keystone, Pennsylvania.

This company greatly altered the mill. The boiler room was enlarged from three boilers to ten, and a large

32

brick chimney was built. It now took ten carloads of coal a day to keep the plant going. Twenty-two charcoal retorts were also built, and these also demanded a goodly amount of coal. Some days as many as thirty carloads of coal came in by the New York Central for the plant.

Also built was a chemical plant for refining the steam from the charcoal retorts, and about forty company houses, plus a company boarding house, on a brand new section called Penny Avenue.

In addition to all this, the new company extended railroad tracks across Black River eastward as far as Brantingham Lake, looking forward to the time when hardwood on the west side would become scarce. This line was known as the Glenfield and Eastern.

The company was controlled by the Quinn family, who also owned and operated the Potato Creek Railroad in Pennsylvania. A large amount of equipment, including several locomotives and railroad cars, was transferred from this line for use on the new railroad, and some were also diverted to the Glenfield and Western. This line was also extended on into Campbell Wood, in the Town of Montague, to get at an added supply of timber.

In the month of July, 1929, the Keystone Company shipped from Glenfield the following: forty-six carloads of lumber, one hundred and six carloads of charcoal, six carloads of acetic acid, three carloads of methanol, and one carload of acetone. It is clear that, had they been able to remain in business, this company would have greatly changed the stature of the village of Glenfield.

As it was, the company probably spread themselves around too much for their own good. Apparently this fact led to their downfall; aided and abetted by the general state of the economy of the nation, which was headed for the big depression. Late in 1929 they were forced into bankruptcy, and all their holdings went into the hands of receivers. The Glenfield plant was torn down and sold for junk, and all the new houses suffered the same fate. So also, apparently, did faithful old No. 22.

The Glenfield and Western continued to operate for six months under the control of the receivers, then its operation also was suspended. In 1931 the rails were taken up and removed to Glenfield by the last struggles for survival by the old line, consuming herself as she went, as it were. From Glenfield they were transferred by truck to Syracuse, where giant shears cut them into sixteen-inch lengths for scrap metal.

On December 16, 1932, Number 75 was bought from the receivers for the sum of one hundred dollars by Frank G. Bates, who had served the line for many years as conductor. Mr. Bates had intended to convert her to scrap metal, but perhaps a sentimental part of his nature prevented him from doing so. On June 16, 1933, he resold her to the Norwood and St. Lawrence Railroad Company, where she continued to give service for many years as No. 213.

Although the Glenfield and Western was primarily a logging railroad, it did accommodate passengers in the caboose of each train. Old records reveal something of the prices charged for this service. From Glenfield to Monteola, the greatest distance, was seventy-five cents; Glenfield to Houseville, twenty-five cents; Monteola to Gulfhead, forty cents; Glenfield to Page, a half dollar. Passengers were also carried on the Jitney in good weather, apparently at the same prices.

The records also give the names of many of the officials and employees. J. C. Humes and Leslie Johnson were the two superintendents. Frank Bates served as conductor. After the demise of the railroad, Mr. Bates served summers as a Lewis County deputy sheriff. During the winters he served as a security officer in the Assembly Chambers in Albany. He would have succeeded to the office of Sergeant-at-Arms the next year after the termination of his service by his untimely death in 1950. Engineers were Charlie Graves and Amos Levings. Mr. Graves still lives in Lowville. Harry Salsburg, Earl Rennie and Royal Austin served as firemen on the two locomotives. Brakemen were J. Rinkenburg, V. Clark, Mord Johnson, J. Quinn, and B. Buker. H. M. Hilts was night watchman around the terminal buildings. There were also a section foreman and seven laborers who kept the right-of-way clean and the tracks as safe as possible, and many in the roundhouse and machine shop crews whose names are, regrettably, not available.

Yes, the old "Gee Whiz" is gone now. The relentless forests have over-run the clearings where her logging camps and hamlets used to be, and are fast encroaching on her right-of-way, part of which now serves as a truck road for logs still coming down from the Hill. Most of her bridges are gone, as are her culverts and cattle passes; her water towers and buildings and depots.

But she is not forgotten by the few old-time residents who knew her in her heyday. Although neither her span of life or her overall length were very great, she served a purpose and served it well. And that makes her as worthy of recognition as any railroad in the land.

And there are still a few whose imaginations doubtless conjure up the deep-throated throb and resounding whistles of her two locomotives echoing among the gulfs and forests of Tug Hill.

THE HIGHWAYS OF WINTER

As has been reiterated time after time in these writings, the winter snows in and around the Tug Hill area were the deepest and longest lasting of any in the whole northeast. They came early, fell heavily, and stayed late. As an example, during February of 1925 there was seven and a half feet of this white insulation protecting the top of the Hill from the far below-zero temperatures. This was a level average, with drifts two and three times that deep.

As can readily be suspected, keeping the highways passable during the winter months was something of a chore. Of course, winter automobile travel in those days was almost unheard of in the rural areas. When the snow reached hub-cap depth, or before, what few cars there were on the farms were carefully put away in garages and barns, with the wheels blocked up to take the weight off the tires. So for a few months the roads were for horse travel alone, and the methods used to keep them passable were meant for that purpose. These methods were not confined to any one area alone, but were more or less prevalent in all northern rural regions.

The simplest of these methods was "kettling out." Nearly every farm owned at least one of the huge old cauldron kettles made of cast iron three-eighths of an inch thick and used for many purposes about the place. After a snowfall a chain was wrapped around the kettle just below the rim and it was dragged down the road behind a single unit of a pair of sleighs, or bobs, as they were known. The round bottom of the kettle made a beautiful track, and when turned around and dragged in the opposite direction created a road easily negotiated by a team and sleighs. A variation of this method was to drag a log in place of the kettle, but the results of either method were highly vulnerable to blowing snow and would drift full in a few hours.

Sometimes a crude snowplow was constructed of heavy hardwood planks and drawn by one or two teams, depending on the depth of the snow. This would clear the snow road width at one passage, but it too had its disadvantage. If the snow was damp and packey, it would push ahead of the plow, gradually building up until it reached the heels of the rearmost team. Then it had to be broken up and thrown out with shovels.

These types of roads, being only one lane wide, required "turning out places," in other words, spots made wider where two teams might meet and pass. It was an unwritten rule that if a loaded team and an unloaded team met, the unloaded team should take to the deep snow on the shoulder and pull around the laden outfit. If two loaded teams met, common courtesy dictated that each should pull far enough off the track to allow passage of the two outfits.

But common courtesy did not always prevail, as is illustrated by a rather amusing tale told about two men who used to live up near Maple Ridge, on the eastern flank of Tug Hill. It seems that these two men, while not really enemies, held a mutual dislike for each other, and both were stiff-necked and stubborn to the last degree. One day they met on a narrow winter road, each hauling a heavy load and each determined to have the right-of-way.

When the heads of the two teams were almost bumping, they stopped of their own volition, and the two drivers sat berating each other and each demanding that the other pull off the road and let him pass. And, of course, both refused.

So there they sat, each stubbornly refusing to give an inch, from before noon until the evening shadows began to fall. Neither had softened an iota, and both were determined to stay all night if necessary. Fortunately, the weather was comparatively mild, so neither the horses or the men suffered from the cold.

Meanwhile, other rigs going in both directions continued to congregate behind them. Those traveling light proceeded to pull around and by them, but the loaded outfits could not do this and after a while the patience of the drivers of these rigs began to wear thin. Many angry words were shouted, along with a few threats, but the two stubborn men refused to budge.

At last an understandably peeved group converged upon the roadblock. A substitute driver climbed upon each rig, took over the lines, and proceeded to pull halfway out of the track and pass in the conventional manner. This of course saved the face of both original drivers; but it was a sad commentary on human nature, and did not win friends for either of them.

By far the most satisfactory method of breaking out winter roads was by rolling. This was accomplished by the use of a huge, ponderous affair known as a snowroller, and drawn by two and sometimes three teams of horses. In reality, it was two rollers, being composed of two hollow wooden cylinders, each about seven feet in diameter and six feet wide, and mounted upon a single horizontal axle that extended through the center of each. The reason for this division was to enable the machine to turn more easily. For instance, if a left-hand turn was desired, the right-hand drum continued its forward motion while the left-hand one turned backward; a rather ingenious arrangement.

The drums were separated on the axle by about two

or three inches, and the axle extended for a foot or more past each end of the drums. Upon these protrusions were mounted two light timbers fitted at the halfway point with bearings in which each axle ran, and which carried two platforms, ahead of and behind the rollers. These were for the drivers of the teams, the position of the drivers corresponding to the positions of their teams. If three teams were used, two drivers used the back platform, thereby using their weight to help counter-balance the weight of the pole, or neap, on the neck-yoke of the rearmost team.

A trip over the road with this ponderous contraption produced a smooth, hard-packed surface a full twelve feet wide, even in snow up to two feet deep. The very best time for rolling was when the snow was slightly packey; then when it froze the track became almost as hard as concrete, and much more slippery. In fact, such a road was almost ideal for sleigh runners, and it did away with the necessity of turning out places.

The drivers of these rollers contracted with the Road Commissioner (Highway Superintendent) to cover a given route, usually eight to ten miles, as many times as the Road Commissioner deemed it necessary, at a stated amount for each trip. It was a cold and uncomfortable task, sometimes in storms and blizzards, but it did produce a superior type of winter road for horse-drawn vehicles.

However, rolling did have one very bad drawback, even though large loads of logs and lumber slipped along with ease on such a track. During the course of a long winter the hard-packed mass of snow and ice would sometimes build up to a depth of from two to three feet, and when the spring "breakup" came and this started to soften up it was impossible to use these roads even for foot travel. Long after plowed and kettled roads had been freed of snow by the warm spring sun, this mass

40

remained adamant, sometimes for two or three weeks. At such times farmers and others who had to use the roads skirted along the edges, or through the fields when necessary.

An interesting side-light on the use of winter roads is the manner in which the horses that traveled them were shod. Teams that were to be used for farm work, skidding logs, breaking out woods roads, or any other chore that required them to travel in deep snow were left dull-shod; which meant, with the same blunt calked shoes as were worn in summer. Sometimes the shoes were taken off entirely during the winter months. But horses that were to be used on iced hauling roads or any other slick surfaces were "sharp-shod," or equipped with shoes having long and sharp toe and heel calks to give them a firm footing and more traction on slippery surfaces. These teams were kept out of deep snow as much as possible, for many horses were inclined to panic under such conditions, and in their wild plunging might severely gash either their own legs or those of their team-mate. Many a good horse has been ruined for life in this manner.

Under certain snow conditions, snow-balls would build up under the hoofs of shod horses. Sometimes these would release themselves before reaching any great size, but at other times they would continue to grow until the horse was walking four or five inches above the road surface. At this size they became dangerous, as they might cause a horse to stumble or roll a foot, with the possible result of straining a tendon. Wise teamsters kept a wary eye out for these hazards, and whenever one was detected the team was stopped and the snowballs knocked loose. Most of them carried a small hammer or wooden mallet for this purpose, usually hung on a hame knob by a cord loop attached to the handle.

As the winter went by the shoulders of the roads became littered with these hard-packed snowballs, and often long after the other snow had melted, the remains of these wintry relics lingered to remind folks of the rigorous months just passed. Many a country lad on his way to school used them for footballs even after the dogtooth violets had begun to bloom.

Today, as people speed along well plowed and sanded roads all winter long in their well-heated automobiles, it is hard to believe that such conditions ever existed.

THE NORTH COUNTRY DAYS
OF FRANK W. WOOLWORTH . . .

The Five-and-Ten, as it is known today, has become as closely woven into the fabric of America's everyday life as the automobile, the television set, and the daily newspaper. In the number of its customers, it almost rivals the stars within man's knowledge of the universe.

Three quarters of a century ago this was not the case. At that time the phrase embraced only a handful of shabby little shops scattered mostly through New York State and Pennsylvania, whose merchandise consisted mostly of pots and pans and small notions, because other articles that could be sold at that cheap price were virtually non-existent. They were smugly ignored by reputable merchants, and even looked down upon by the small segment of the public which they served.

Today, there are thousands of five-and-tens in many lands. Although they have increased the latitude of their merchandise and advanced their prices, thereby becoming serious competitors of large department stores, their basic appeal remains the same: the wondrous purchasing power of these small segments of the dollar.

Most great ideas are simple, and usually can be traced to an individual who believes in, and tenaciously clings to the pursuit of, an impossible dream. Thomas A. Edison was an example of this. So were Alexander Graham Bell, Henry Ford, and the Wright Brothers. So also was Frank Winfield Woolworth, who believed implicitly in the future of the five-and-ten cent store, and who won out over incredible obstacles.

43

The first twenty-one years of Woolworth's life were passed on farms in Jefferson County, on the northeast shoulder of the Tug Hill Plateau. In that region, then as now, the winters were long and rigorous, the summers seemingly short. On almost any morning from December to April a path had to be shoveled from the house to the barn, after which hay had to be thrown down for the cattle, the stables cleaned, and the cows milked. To Frank and his younger brother, Sumner, nothing seemed so cold and disagreeable as the handles of those shovels and pitchforks. The milking chore was a little more agreeable, for at this they could at least get their hands warm.

Charles Sumner Woolworth, Frank's brother and the only other child in the family, many years later recalled those days on the backwoods farm.

"Spring came late up there near Rodman and Great Bend," he reminisced. "Frank and I each had only one pair of rough cowhide boots a year. In May, when we started following a peg-toothed harrow over that rough, stony soil, the boots were pretty well worn and the seams would open up and let in lots of dirt, which had to be shaken out every now and then. So we started going barefoot as soon as possible.

"In the summer the weather became pretty hot and we labored long hours in the hayfields, putting away fodder for the next winter. The worst job was storing it away in the hot, airless peak of the barn. In September we many times had to go barefooted to hunt up the cows at five o'clock in the morning when the ground was white with frost, and when we found them we used to stand on the spots where cows had been lying to get a little warmth into our nearly frozen feet.

"In late October we would pick up potatoes, one of our main crops, until our backs were breaking and our fingers were numb with cold and encrusted with dirt. No

44

wonder we longed to break away from the endless drudgery of the farm."

The surname Woolworth was the American adaptation of an ancient English locality designation. As far back as the thirteenth century there were numerous Woleys, Wolleys, and Woolys scattered throughout southern England. The early colonial representative of the family, Richard, who was a weaver, was known as Wolley, as well as Woolworth, in the records of Newbury, Massachusetts, where he landed in 1678. During the ensuing years his descendants spread throughout New England and upper New York State, married locally, and raised large families. For the most part they were frugal, industrious, God-fearing people.

The early 1840's found Richard's great-great-grandson, Jasper, farming what was known as the old Moody place, in the Town of Rodman, Jefferson County. He was aided by his son, John Hubble Woolworth, who was born August 16, 1821.

On nearby Pillar Point, a peninsula extending out into Lake Ontario, lived Henry McBrier with his wife and eight children. The McBriers had come to America in 1825 from County Down, Ireland, and like the Woolworths were staunch Methodists. One of the McBrier daughters caught the fancy of young John, and the entire neighborhood agreed that he was indeed a lucky fellow when the black-haired, blue-eyed Fanny consented to become his bride. They were married on the fourteenth of January, 1851.

A short distance from the main house on Jasper Woolworth's farm there stood a small cottage, and here John and Fanny set up housekeeping. Here were born their two sons. Frank Winfield first saw the light of day April 13, 1852, and Charles Sumner followed some four years later, on August 1, 1856. Charles Sumner was named for that eminent abolitionist whose anti-slavery

45

views the Woolworths and McBriers shared and supported. Frank Winfield was merely a euphoneus combination that happened to appeal to the fancy of the parents.

In the year 1858, Father Woolworth sold his farm at
Rodman, and his son John had to find a new home for
his family. After considerable searching he finally purchased a farm near Great Bend, also in Jefferson County and about thirteen miles from Watertown. The village was named for the wide sweeping bend made by
Black River in that area.

A colorful character of bygone days in the region had
been Joseph Bonaparte, the erstwhile King of Spain and
brother of Napoleon, who early in the century had built
a home for his mistress, Ann Savage, on the Indian
River near Great Bend. A little farther away was Lake
Bonaparte, where stood ex-King Joe's sumptuous hunting lodge. Here he and his followers would float on this
beautiful body of water in a great Venetian-style gon-
dola while they fished and ate and drank, and sang as
they dreamed of the future Napoleonic empire that they
would establish in the great north country after they had
rescued Napoleon from St. Helena. Their plan was to
bring him to Cape Vincent, a few miles north of Watertown, where they had actually built a house for his residence. This was called the Cup-and-Saucer House, because of its appearance. But unfortunately for their in-
tentions, their plans failed, and Napoleon was never
able to make an appearance in northern New York.

Young Frankie Woolworth used to sit and listen in
rapture to tales of the grandeur enjoyed by these French
noblemen, never dreaming that someday he himself
would bask in the wonders of a self-created empire
every bit as resplendent as that of Napoleon himself.

John Woolworth, however, was more concerned with
the problem of making ends meet. A sixteen hundred
dollar mortgage on the farm carried an interest rate of

seven per cent, which twice a year necessitated a payment of fifty-six dollars. Fanny Woolworth had taken upon herself the responsibility of seeing that there was money to pay this, and saving for the next installment began almost immediately after the current one was paid.

The Woolworth family knew no holidays. Even Sunday was only a partial day of rest. The Methodist Church in the village was their only social outlet. John Woolworth and his wife both sang in the choir, while Frank and "Sum" washed and polished until they shone and dressed in their Sunday best, attended Sunday-school. But as soon as the family had returned from meeting, off came the good clothes and the rest of the day was devoted to attending to various farm chores.

Frankie had attended the little red schoolhouse at Rodman, and continued his schooling at Great Bend, where the terms were short. A former teacher commented on his deportment while he was a pupil in this school.

"Frankie Woolworth was always a good scholar," she said. "He was well behaved and never gave me the least trouble. He was also exceptionally bright and serious-minded, never prankish, and always had his lessons. He was a good looking boy and pleasant in disposition."

Frank Woolworth grew up tall and thin, and not overly robust. He was nimble-witted, and always persistent in following through and completing whatever he undertook to do. He had a decided penchant for decorative effect, and as evidence of this he tore down the old rail fence around the house and replaced it with a neat picket one. He also landscaped the yard with shrubs and saplings transplanted from the nearby forests.

One of his dearest possessions during this period of his life was a flute. This was the first of the various instruments upon which, during most of his life, he attempted to express himself. But although music was a

47

lifelong obsession, musical expression was never to be his. The truth of the matter was that he had absolutely no sense of pitch, and was never able to even carry a tune.

Although his entire family, and in fact most of the surrounding countryside, were pro-Lincoln and keenly abolitionist, the Civil War, which occurred during Frankie's most formative years, aroused in him no yearning for military glories. In fact, the holocaust of the conflict raging in Pennsylvania, Maryland and Virginia seemed somewhat remote to many people in the north country. But they all remembered the rejoicing that came with the news of Lee's surrender; and no one could ever forget the sense of helpless rage and horror that attended the news of Lincoln's assassination.

At the age of sixteen, Frank Woolworth's schooling was apparently over, and he began to put in full time on the farm. More than ever before he came to detest the dull monotony of farm work, and his determination to break away from it increased day by day. In this purpose he had a staunch ally, his mother. Little by little she saved up enough money to enable him to take two short courses in a school of commerce in Watertown.

When these were completed, Frank set out to find a job. The highest position at which he could aim was to become a clerk in some store, and he felt that he would be perfectly satisfied with this for a start. So he harnessed a horse to the family cutter and set out for Carthage, a village of about fifteen hundred people twelve miles east of Great Bend. Here were situated a small collection of stores, including a furniture and undertaking establishment, a meat market, and a grocery. He visited each business place in turn, asking for work. But no one felt that they needed a green country lad, and he returned home deeply disheartened.

Although the young man did not realize it, he was

the victim of an economic condition that was severely out of joint. Financial interests were still staggering under the strain brought on by several years of war. A gold dollar was worth a dollar and a half to two dollars in paper money. Prices were high. Few women could afford to pay twenty-five cents a yard for print calico, or forty cents a yard for unbleached muslin. Other prices were comparatively high, and the result was stagnant trade.

Finally, Daniel McNiel, who ran the small general store at Great Bend, called Frank into the store one day.

"Frankie, I want to make you a proposition," he announced. "On rush days I need help sometimes, and you could come in and give me a hand, but I can't afford to pay you any wages. But you would be getting experience in clerking and dealing with people, and I would keep my ears open when I am in Watertown and try to find an opening for you there. What do you say?"

Frank accepted eagerly, and on the days when he worked in the store he did his best to please the kind-hearted storekeeper. He also kept his eyes and ears open to learn everything he could about the business. But in February of 1873, his uncle, Arvin McBrier, offered him eighteen dollars a month, with board and lodging, to work on his farm. His father thought that he should not refuse it, as it was a sure thing, whereas a job in a store was very nebulous to say the least. But the thoughts of continuing farm work filled Frank with loathing, and he begged for a little more time before making up his mind.

He was now almost twenty-one, and it was time that he made a definite break for himself. His brother was old enough to take his place on the family farm, and he was not sorely needed there. Somewhat desperately he pinned his hopes on the promise of Daniel McNiel to try to help him get situated in a store job. They were anxious days. Time was running out on his uncle's offer, and he had to make his decision soon. Nearly every night he went to ask the kindly storekeeper if there was any news, and one night he was rewarded. McNiel had been into Watertown that day on a buying trip, and he greeted Frank with a big smile.

"Say Frankie, there's an opening for a clerk at Augsbury and Moore's," he announced. "I heard about it today. I know Augsbury and I'll give you a letter to him. Maybe you can get the job."

This company, located on the American corner of the Public Square, was one of the leading dry goods stores of Watertown. A chance with them seemed at the moment to represent the very height of Frank Woolworth's ambition, and to say that he was elated would be putting it mildly.

Early the next morning he arrived at the store, eager to be there before any other applicant could beat him out of his chance. Upon inquiry he learned that Mr. Augsbury was at home sick, so he inquired where the gentleman lived and made his way there.

"So you want a job," said Augsbury, after reading Mr. McNiel's letter. Quickly his practiced glance took in the tall, gangling country lad, the thick cowhide boots, rough work shirt, and home-knit scarf that he wore in place of an overcoat. "Do you drink? Do you smoke? What do you do that's bad?" Woolworth replied that he neither drank nor smoked, and that as far as he knew he didn't do anything that was very bad.

"Well, you look too green to me, and you've had no experience," declared Augsbury. "But I'll tell you what. You go and see Mr. Moore, and if he thinks it's alright, we'll put you to work. But only on a trial basis, mind you."

So Frank went back to the store to talk with the other partner. William H. Moore, although only twelve years Frank's senior, was an imposing figure to the lanky

50

country boy. Dressed in the very height of business fashion and wearing bushy side whiskers, he sat at a big desk on a raised platform and gazed down with a slightly annoyed look on his face. When informed of Mr. Augsbury's decision, he promptly put the youth through an interrogation that left him in a slightly dazed condition.

"Why do you want to leave the farm?" he asked. "Don't you know that the hours in a store are long and the work is hard? If we take you on you will have to do all the heavy and dirty work that needs to be done. You'll have to get here early and clean the whole store, even wash the spitoons. It will be the hardest work that you ever did in your life."

But Frank was determined not to let all this discouraging talk rob him of his big chance.

"I'm not afraid of hard work, sir," he said. "And the reason I want to leave the farm is to gain experience in the merchandising business. If you hire me you will find me a good worker. How much are you going to pay me?"

Moore looked shocked. "Pay you?" he said. "Why, you'd ought to pay us for teaching you the business. If you go to school to learn a trade you have to pay tuition. Well, we won't charge you any tuition fee, but you'll have to work for nothing until we decide if you are worth anything, and if so, how much."

Frank's heart sank clear to his boots. "How long will that take?" he asked. Moore had a ready answer. "At least six months," he snapped.

If ever Frank Woolworth stood at a crossroads, it was at that moment. His disappointment was intense, almost overpowering. But so was his determination, bolstered as it was by his loathing of the many years of frustrating work on the farm. Quickly he made a mental assessment of the situation, and after a few cerebral gymnastics he proposed a compromise.

"Mr. Moore," he said, "I have about fifty dollars

that I have earned at odd jobs. I figure that it will pay for my board and lodging here in Watertown for about three months. I will work for nothing for the first three months if you will agree to pay me three dollars and fifty cents a week for the second three months."

Moore considered this proposal with a slightly amused expression on his face and just a hint of a twinkle in his eye. Apparently he was somewhat impressed by the spunk of this country bumpkin who would stand up to him and make such a counter-offer. Although his mind was already made up, he still went through the formality of discussing the matter. The upshot of the discussion was that the new employee should come to work on the terms that he had proposed on the following Monday morning, March 24, 1873.

Frankie asked if he could be a little late on that first morning, explaining that his father was coming into the city with a load of potatoes, and that by riding in with the potatoes he could save thirty-three cents railroad fare. Moore reluctantly said that he thought that would be alright and, highly elated, Frank started for home to share the good news with the family.

Throughout a long and eventful life, Frank Woolworth never forgot the scene at the little farm near Great Bend on that frosty March morning when he set out to make his way in the world. The night before a deep layer of straw had been laid in the bottom of the sleigh, to serve as insulation against the cold that came up from below, and on this they placed the potatoes, barrel after barrel and bag upon bag. Spaces were left between the barrels to accommodate lighted oil lanterns, in hopes that they would give off enough heat to keep the potatoes from freezing. Over them all were spread all available horse blankets, lap robes and bran sacks.

As they pulled away from the house, Frank's mother and brother stood in the open kitchen door, the lamplight behind them, waving their hands and calling, "Goodbye, Frankie, Goodbye." It may well be presumed that this home-loving country boy, now leaving home for the first time, had an unaccustomed lump in his throat and perhaps tears in his eyes as he waved back as long as he could see the house.

Of course the start was made long before daylight, and the air fairly sparkled with frost. The breath of men and animals rose in clouds of steam as they made their way along the street of Great Bend. Here and there the feeble light of a lantern punched a small hole in the darkness as some early riser went about his affairs, and now and then the barking of a dog drifted to them on the still air.

As the dawn broke, the cold increased, and soon it became necessary for father and son to get off and walk behind the sleigh to keep up their circulation. But as the sun rose higher, so did the temperature, and by the time they had reached Watertown a beautiful winter day had developed. A day, young Woolworth hoped, propitious to his first adventure into the world of merchandising.

But before noon of that day, he was not so sure that this was going to be so. Mr. Augsbury was the first one that he encountered upon entering the store, and this gentleman looked him over critically.

"Don't they wear collars and ties where you come from?" he asked abruptly.

"No sir, at least not while we are working," replied Frank.

"And is that flannel shirt the best that you have to wear?"

Again Woolworth replied in the affirmative.

"Well, you'd better go out and get yourself a white shirt, collar, and tie before you go to work," said Mr. Augsbury testily.

53

Although this cut severely into the capital upon which he had to depend for three months, Frank proceeded to comply with the order. Soon after he returned properly rigged out, Mr. Augsbury left the store for lunch, or dinner as it was then known. Nobody had told the young man what to do, and he stood around feeling rather foolish. The clerks in the store sneered at him and offered no sign of friendship, and he felt that they were considering him to be an awkward clod. And this, they afterward told him, was just what they were thinking.

Somewhat desperately, in search of something to do, Woolworth moved behind a counter, and soon after a farmer came in and approached him.

"Young man, I want a spool of thread," he requested.

Frank did not know where they kept the thread, so he went over to where Mr. Moore was busy behind his desk, and asked him.

"Right in front of your nose, young man," snapped Mr. Moore, without looking up.

Frank went back and pulled out a drawer directly in front of where he stood, and sure enough, it was filled with spools of thread.

"I want number forty," said the customer.

Up until that time, Frank did not know that thread had a number. Although he searched diligently he could not locate the kind desired, so he had to appeal to Mr. Moore again, who told him that it was right there in the drawer. Somewhat diffidently, Frank told him that he could not find it.

"Just as I thought,' said Moore disgustedly, as he climbed down from his desk and came over to find the right spool of thread.

"How much is it?" the farmer asked.

Frank of course did not know, and again he had to

appeal to Mr. Moore. It was eight cents, and the man handed him a ten-cent "shin-plaster."

Note: During the Civil War silver coins had practically disappeared, so in place of them the government issued fractional currency dubbed "shin-plasters" by a facetious public. These were issued in the amounts of three cents, five cents, ten cents, fifteen cents, twenty-five cents, and fifty cents. In 1875 Congress enacted a law calling for the replacement of fractional currency by silver coins "as rapidly as possible," and the redemption of all shin-plasters by hard money on demand, after January 1, 1879.

"Mr. Moore, where do I get change?" he had to ask.

"Come right up to the desk and make out a ticket," Moore said.

Frank picked up one of the blanks and studied it, but could not make up his mind what to do with it.

"Mr. Moore, I dont' believe I know how to make this out," he had to confess.

"Hand it to me and I'll show you," said the long-suffering Moore. This he proceeded to do, then returned to his work.

"But where do I get my change?" Frank persisted.

"There is the cashier right there. Can't you see him?"

Frank presented the slip to the cashier and received two cents change. All this had been observed with a good deal of amusement by the other clerks in the establishment, but no one offered assistance. Frank felt like sinking through the floor, but his persistence and determination bolstered him up. Although he felt like quitting the job then and there, he knew that such a defeatist attitude would never get him anywhere in his chosen profession.

That was Frank W. Woolworth's first sale, and although he and his organization made millions of them after that, this was the one that he would remember all his life.

Soon after this another customer entered the store and asked to buy a pair of mittens. As usual, Frank did not know where to look, so once again he had to interrupt Mr. Moore.

"Mr. Moore, do we have any mittens?" he asked.

"Right there in front of you," Moore snapped. Frank looked, and sure enough there they were, a whole selection of them. The farmer looked them over carefully and finally selected a pair.

"How much?" he asked. Frank did not know.

"Mr. Moore, how much are these mittens?" he asked.

By this time Moore was becoming well fed up by these continual interruptions from his new apprentice.

"Look on the price tag. Look on the price tag," he shouted. "The price is right there on the tag."

Sure enough, the price of twenty-five cents was plainly written on the tag. The man paid with a dollar bill, and this time Frank knew how to make out the slip and where to get change, so he did not have to bother Mr. Moore again. In spite of his discouraging start, he felt that he was making some progress.

The next day went better. The new man left his boarding house early and had the store cleaned and polished until it shone before either of the owners arrived. Even the cuspidors were thoroughly washed and polished. After that he had packages to deliver, and heavy boxes to handle and unpack in the stockroom. He did everything that he could to make himself useful, but he was finding out that store work was, indeed, hard work. All the time he kept his eyes and ears open in an endeavor to learn all he could about the business.

In spite of themselves, the other employees were impressed by his courtesy, his cheerfulness, and his evident

56

willingness to work, and gradually they began to unthaw. One of the first of these was E. W. Barrett, the ♪ head clerk, who was earning the princely salary of thirteen dollars a week. Mr. Barrett was quick to recognize the fact that Frank was intelligent, and quick and eager to learn. Another sympathetic soul was Mrs. A. E. Coons, a stout and matronly lady clerk whose kindness to Woolworth was never forgotten. These two, together with a few others, helped him over many a rough spot.

The only opportunity that Frank had to work behind a counter was during the noon hour while the other clerks were at lunch. One noon a Mr. Merrill, from Franks' home area, came into the store and asked to be personally waited upon by the young man. This, of course, puffed up his ego somewhat, and he stepped behind a counter with an assumed air of confidence. Mr. Merrill wanted ten yards of calico for his wife, and although he had no idea of how to measure off ten yards of the material, Frank picked up a bolt of cloth and began to unroll it. He found the material very slippery, and soon a veritable deluge of calico was billowing over the counter and down onto the floor.

Mr. Moore looked up from his desk, saw what was going on, and uttered one agonized word, "Stop," after which he came down to wait on the customer himself. This taught Frank a valuable lesson; never be overconfident.

One afternoon about four, as Frank was passing Mr. Moore's desk, the store owner said without raising his eyes, "Woolworth, take all the goods out of the front window and give it a good washing." As Frank moved away to comply he added, "And when you've done that, dress the window again."

The young man was elated; this was real store work, he thought. Forgetting about supper, he worked far into the night. He helped himself liberally to remnants of different fabrics in the store for background effects, sticking to a red theme wherever possible. Other merchandise from the store was also used, and he arranged and rearranged the articles dozens of times before they finally pleased his artistic taste, and he went home to bed.

When Mr. Moore arrived at the store the next morning, he paused for a long minute inspecting the window, while Woolworth lingered nearby with his broom. Typically, the store owner made no direct comment one way or the other, but he never did when he was satisfied, so Frank concluded that perhaps he had done well. And this must have been the case, for from that time on, the job of window-dressing always fell to him.

And so he went on, striving, learning, improving. At the end of three months he received his promised three dollars and fifty cents a week, was raised to four dollars at six months, and finally at the end of a year was raised again to six dollars a week. Now earning a dollar for each working day, he began to feel like a millionaire. Long ago, he had discarded his heavy scarf and replaced it with an overcoat, and now he bought himself a tall silk hat. This he first wore to church on Easter morning.

No one was now any more pleased with himself than was Frank Woolworth, but the other boarders at his boarding house continued to have fun at his expense. Without realizing it, he was far from the sophisticated man of the world that he imagined himself to be. For a long time he had practiced on his flute, but now despairing of ever mastering it, he changed to a violin, on which he also practiced industriously. The other boarders wished that he would change back to the flute, as the violin proved far more abrasive to the nerves.

About this time Mr. Augsbury, the senior partner in the store, sold out his interest to a man named Smith, and the firm now became Moore and Smith. Mr. Smith sized up the help and quickly came to the conclusion

58

that while clerk Woolworth was a bust as a salesman, clerk Woolworth was good at cataloging merchandise and arranging displays.

This latter opinion was also the opinion of clerk Woolworth, who began to believe that he was worth more money. So when the position of head clerk became vacant in the rival store of A. Bushnell & Co. he applied for it. As he entered the store and observed the untidy condition of counters and displays, he made a mental note of what an improvement he could make here. When Mr. Bushnell asked what salary he expected, Frank boldly replied,

"I think I am worth ten dollars a week, sir." To his great surprise Mr. Bushnell replied, "That will be satisfactory."

Moore and Smith were just as surprised when they heard the news, but they made no offer to meet that salary, so Woolworth went to work for Bushnell. One of the requirements of the new job was that he would sleep in the basement to attend the furnace and protect the store from burglars. He was given a revolver and a companion, a gay and jolly lad named Harry Moody, who also slept at the store. The two soon became fast friends, but little did they dream as they lay on their cots in Bushnell's basement that they would one day be associated in a sixty-five million dollar enterprise that would revolutionize the accepted concept of merchandising.

Mr. Bushnell did not share Moore and Smith's ideas of the importance of sprucing up the store, and resisted all Frank's efforts to improve the decor. What he wanted was not a decorator but a salesman, and salesmanship was still Woolworth's weak point. One day the store owner told him bluntly that he had six-dollar-a-week boys selling far more goods than he was, and that his salary would have to be reduced to eight dollars a week.

Woolworth accepted the cut in salary as gracefully

as possible, but it started him on a long period of depression that grew deeper and deeper. Harry Moody did his cheery best to bolster the spirits of his friend, but it did no good. Though he continued to work as hard as ever, he grew more thin and wan day by day. Finally he went to see a doctor, who told him that he was too weak to work, and advised him to go back to the farm to recuperate.

Another young man named Carlton Peck was put in his place temporarily, as it was thought that his recovery would be speedy. But this did not prove to be the case. For weeks Frank lay in a state of almost complete physical and mental collapse, and his despondency grew. The chance for success in a mercantile career seemed to be lost forever.

Long months of sleeping in Bushnell's basement, coupled with hard work, long hours, and indifferent boarding house food, had contributed physically to his breakdown. But another and deeper cause added to his depression and slowed his recovery. Frank Woolworth was in love.

While working in Watertown he had met a young Canadian girl from Picton, Ontario, who had come to the city to earn her living as a seamstress. Her name was Jenny Creighton, and the circumstances of her family were, if anything, even more humble than those of the Woolworths. But she often became very lonely for her own folks, and she and Frank immediately took to one another, being as they were, kindred spirits. Gradually their friendship had ripened into something much deeper, and Frank had proposed and been accepted. It was the thought that he would probably now lose Jenny that added to his deep depression.

But Jenny turned out to be the kind of girl who wasn't easily lost. As often as possible she visited the Woolworth farmhouse, and her bright and cheerful personal-

60

ity did wonders for the young man's rehabilitation. Little by little he began to plan again for the future. Even though his chances for success in the mercantile world were lost, would she, he wondered, become a farmer's wife? When he finally summoned up the courage to ask her, it took no time at all for her to make up her mind. She would.

And so on June 11, 1876, they were married in the parlor of the Woolworth farmhouse. The young couple were virtually penniless. After looking about the young groom found a four-acre farm that they could buy for nine hundred dollars, so after signing a note for three hundred dollars, and taking out a mortgage for six hundred dollars, the newly married couple moved in their few belongings. The house was a little run down at the heel, but they were able to fix it up until it was fairly comfortable, and best of all, they were together.

On their new farm they raised chickens, potatoes, pigs, and anything else that they could sell. They managed to make a living, but little more, and Frank was restless and dissatisfied. His aversion for farming still remained, and he felt that he should be doing something more meaningful with his life; something that would enable him to provide for Jenny the things that he wanted her to have.

This went on for almost half a year, and then one day Frank received a letter from his old employer, W. H. Moore in Watertown. Moore had learned that window dressing was definitely good for business, and he now offered Frank ten dollars a week to return to his old job. This seemed like a God-sent second chance to the young man, but he was now encumbered with a farm. Far into the night he and Jenny discussed the situation, and at last practical Jenny solved the problem in her own capable way.

"You go back to the store, Frank," she said, "and

I'll stay here and look after the farm." It was a courageous decision for the young woman to make, as she had never before lived on a farm, much less taken on the responsibility of running it herself. But after talking it over it was decided that this was the thing to do.

So the next Monday morning found Woolworth back in his old place in Moore and Smith's store in Watertown, and living in his old boarding house again. Every second weekend he managed to get home to spend Sunday, and to help out what he could with the farm. Thus almost a year passed, and although the life must have proved very distasteful to her, Jenny Woolworth never complained. After all, she was giving her husband a chance to make good in his chosen work, and she had great faith that he would not waste the opportunity, and that her trust in him would be vindicated.

However, in the fall of 1877 a neighbor offered to trade a second hand sewing machine for their chickens, and Frank quickly accepted. They rented out the little farm, and moved their meager possessions into the wing of a house at 238 Franklin Street, in Watertown. After a year of almost continual separation, this seemed like heaven to them, and they wondered if such luck could last. To add to they joy, Jenny was expecting a blessed event.

In the middle of the winter they received word that Frank's mother, who had always been a champion of his cause, was seriously ill. Frank and Jenny rushed to Great Bend and were at her side when she died February 15, 1878. Frank's father and brother, Sumner, were now at their wits end as to what to do. Sumner was as determined as Frank had been to break away from the farm, and Frank now used his influence with Moore and Smith to find a place for him in the store. A housekeeper was hired to keep the old home place and look after the father.

62

Late in the spring of 1878, business in the store dropped to a very low level, and Frank was forced to take a cut in salary to eight dollars and a half a week. This was a bad blow to the young couple, as their first daughter, Helena, was born a few weeks later. But, as was typical of her, Jenny Woolworth made do with less, and helped to tide the family over the rough spots.

One day when business was very slow, a young man exuding an air of prosperity entered the store. This was none other than Golding, the chief clerk at Bushnell's whom Woolworth had replaced. He asked how business was going, and Mr. Moore replied gloomily,

"Slow, very slow. In fact I haven't seen it so bad in twenty years at least."

"I'm sorry to hear that," said Golding. "Why don't you put on a cut-rate sale to stimulate business?"

"A cut-rate sale?" asked Moore, who had never heard of such a thing. "What kind of business is that?"

"You mean you never heard of a five-cent counter?" exclaimed Golding, and went on to explain. "A few months ago a merchant that I know was offered a consignment of men's handkerchiefs that normally sold for twenty-five cents at a price which enabled him to sell them for five cents. He put them on a special counter and folks gobbled them up like hot-cakes. And in the meantime they bought a lot of other goods from his store. Such a sale gets people into your place of business, Mr. Moore. Why don't you try it?"

"Perhaps I shall," said Moore slowly, but with no great show of enthusiasm. Frank Woolworth listened to the conversation eagerly. To him it seemed like a great idea, and he continued to bring the matter up as often as possible. Moore said little about it, but in August when he went to New York on a buying trip he went to Spellman Brothers and ordered a hundred dollars worth of five-cent goods. These included steel pens, crochet hooks, button hooks, watch keys, combs, book straps, safety pins, collar buttons, tin pans, wash basins, turkey red napkins, thimbles, stationery, and harmonicas. The goods arrived the week before the start of the County Fair, then as now held in Watertown.

Of course the task of arranging the display fell to Frank Woolworth, and he went about it eagerly. Utilizing two old sewing tables about six feet long and two feet wide, he arranged a counter running down the center aisle of the store, on which he arranged the merchandise. Over this he hung a large sign proclaiming: "Any article on this counter, 5 cents."

The sale took place the opening day of the fair, and it proved to be one of the banner days of Woolworth's life. Public Square was crowded with people from the surrounding countryside, and most of them had at least a little money to spend. Word spread swiftly about the five-cent bargains at Moore and Smith's, and by nightfall the five-cent counter was bare, and people stood about demanding more goods.

Moore immediately sent off a telegram to Spellman Brothers asking them to rush a duplicate order of goods to him, and it was Woolworth who pounded up the stairs to dispatch the wire from the telegraph office three flights above. He was dog-tired from the strenuous day, but so excited that he scarcely realized it. Moore also was elated, not only because of the success of the sale, but also because people had bought a lot of other merchandise in the meantime.

When the new order arrived, it was sold as quickly and easily as the first. This then, was the first authentic five-cent counter of diversified stock in history, and the people of Watertown were proud that it had happened right there on their own American Corner.

The new concept of merchandising quickly caught on, and was taken up by many local merchants. Many

64

individuals also converted their barns or front rooms into improvised shops, and bought stocks of the cheap articles that could be rapidly reconverted into cash at a small profit. Moore and Smith became wholesalers as well as retailers for this type of merchandise, and for a time did a rushing business.

But reputable merchants laughed at the whole business as a passing fad, and predicted that it would soon die out. As the saturation point began to be reached locally, this appeared to be true. But Frank Woolworth did not believe this. His faith in the five-cent business was implicit, and his fondest dream was to own a five-cent store of his own.

With this in mind he began to explore the possibility of doing so. Mr. Moore told him that it would require at least a capital of three hundred dollars to open such a store, and although this seemed a stupendous amount, he set about trying to raise it. He approached his uncle Julius McBrier for a loan of that amount, but this gentleman, being of Scotch-Irish descent, refused him flatly, labeled the scheme a hare-brained idea, and advised him to stick to his job.

His next step was to approach Moore and Smith with the request that they stake him to three hundred dollars worth of merchandise, with only his note for security. By this time Mr. Moore had come to have complete faith in Frank's integrity and foresight, and the firm agreed to comply with this request.

When he started out on that cold January day in 1879 to find a location for his first store, Woolworth knew that the surrounding territory in Jefferson and Lewis counties had been pretty well exploited and the five-cent craze was on the decline, so he had to search farther afield. None of the villages between Watertown and Rome suited his purpose, so he pushed on to Utica. Here he found to his surprise that this city of thirty-five thousand souls was virtually untouched by the five-cent idea.

After searching about he found a hole-in-the-wall shop that he decided would do. It took a great deal of haggling with the landlord before a rental price that he thought he could afford was agreed upon, but this was finally accomplished. Woolworth afterwards said that he wore a path in front of the telegraph office before he could get up the courage to send a wire to Moore and Smith, instructing them to send on the shipment of goods that he had previously selected. But he finally did so, and the next day he cleaned and rearranged the shop to suit his taste. When the shipment arrived he single-handed arranged it on the counters. While waiting he had bought a few necessities such as wrapping paper, string, and a few article for his bookkeeping. He had also had a large sign bearing the legend "The Great 5-Cent Store" painted, and with this fastened to the front of the shop, he was ready for business.

The grand opening occurred on the evening of Saturday, February 22, 1879; and although this event caused no great ripple in the placid flow of life on Bleeker Street, it did herald the birth of the first real five-cent store in history. And the little ripple that it did cause was destined to grow into a tidal wave of mammoth proportions.

With his departure from his old home territory in northern New York our interest in the day to day doings of Frank Winfield Woolworth ceases. But history has recorded what happened to him and his brain-child after that; how he opened store after store, mostly in New York and Pennsylvania, in the immediate years that followed; how he retained the ones that were successful and closed the ones that were not before they had a chance to do him much financial harm; how he learned that aggressive buying was the key to successful selling;

how his persistent efforts finally enabled him to cut through the barriers of rock-bound tradition and buy his merchandise direct from the manufacturer, thus cutting out the profits of middlemen wholesalers and passing the savings on to his customers in lower prices; how he made every failure a lesson that guided him on to bigger and better things in the future; how he never forgot those who had befriended him in his lean years, nor failed to reward them whenever the opportunity offered.

His was a real-life rags-to-riches story unsurpassed by even the fictitious ones of Horatio Alger. From that one dingy little shop in Utica, which incidentally failed and was closed within three months, he went on to establish a Goliath among the mercantile giants of the world; one that in 1918, one year prior to his death, owned and operated 1,037 stores in many countries, and grossed over one hundred and seven million dollars in sales during the year. It was estimated that over a billion people had entered Woolworth stores during that year.

As has been said, Woolworth's devotion to his friends of his early years became a tradition. Whenever he needed an especially reliable man to place in a position of responsibility, he traveled north to Watertown, where he picked one from among his relatives or former associates. His brother Sumner joined him early and helped him build the organization. He was an astute judge of human nature and behavior, and almost every one of his choices came through with flying colors, eventually to become directors of the company.

Mrs. A. E. Coons, the lady clerk in Augsbury and Moore's, who had befriended the lanky country lad during his first trying days in the store, was made the first lady manager of a Woolworth store, a post which she filled with great success.

And Harry A. Moody, the youthful companion of Frank's days and nights in Bushnell's, was later made the manager of the Rochester store; eventually to be transferred to the New York office as European buyer, and in the end a member of the board of directors. Mr. Moody later established a large agricultural complex near Port Ontario. He died a multi-millionaire.

On one of his trips to Watertown, Woolworth visited his old mentor, William Moore, at the store on the American Corner. He found the store in a state of disrepair, with business bad and Mr. Moore deep in discouragement. Immediateiy he offered to stock the store with merchandise, in gratefulness for Moore's kindness to him in the past. The store owner accepted gratefully, and Woolworth wired to have a generous supply of goods sent. The store was reopened as "Moore's Five and Ten Cent Store," and did business for many years.

After Mr. Moore's death in 1916, Woolworth immediately purchased the site of the old Corner Store and arranged to have a six-story edifice built in its place in honor of William H. Moore. Due to America's entry into World War I the building was not completed until 1921, two years after Woolworth's own death. This building still stands, and for over forty years the ground floor was devoted to a Woolworth store. At present the Watertown Woolworth store is housed in a grandiose new building one block west on Arsenal Street. From it is dispensed an infinite variety of merchandise from the four corners of the earth.

Consistent with his grateful open-handedness to his benefactors, Woolworth did not forget the little village that had been his boyhood home. On September 15, 1915, he presented to the village of Great Bend a beautiful little church, dedicated to the memory of his father and mother, John Hubble and Fanny McBrier Woolworth. In addition he also presented an endowment of twenty thousand dollars in five per cent bonds to provide for the upkeep of the church throughout the years. The church still stands, a credit to the community.

Early in the twentieth century, Woolworth began to toy with the idea of creating another monument, this one to himself, that would endure long after his own time. This dream gradually evolved itself into the erection of a stupendous office building. By this time Woolworth's fortunes had reached a point where to decide upon a course of action was to do it. Architects were consulted, plans were drawn, a site on Broadway in downtown New York was purchased, and construction began. As the giant building rose story after story above the surrounding structures, Woolworth's delight in his creation increased.

On the twenty-fourth floor of the mammoth building, Woolworth established his office quarters in a palatial suite of rooms. His own private office was large enough to acommodate three or four of conventional size, and was called the Empire Room. In arranging the appointments of this room he had harked back to the tales of Napoleonic splendor that he had marveled at as a lad, and the room had been fashioned after one in the Royal Palace at Compiegne. Almost as lavish were the offices of the lesser officials of the company, which adjoined the Empire Room.

At exactly seven thirty on the evening of April 24, 1913, President Woodrow Wilson pressed a button in the White House in Washington, and immediately the towering Woolworth building in New York became a column of dazzling light. Proclaimed to be the tallest building in the world, the monolithic giant rose to the impressive height of seven hundred and ninety-two feet and one inch, with its foundation reaching one hundred and twenty-one feet below the sidewalk to bed rock. Never had such a sight been seen in New York or, in fact, all the world. Only the Eiffel Tower was taller, and that was not a building.

An anecdote aptly portraying Woolworth's reluctance to allow anyone to outdo him in anything was related by Frank Cass, the organist in the great building. As the upper floors of the goliath were completed, their proud owner explored them eagerly. One day as he was showing Mr. Cass about, the two men had gone as far up as elevators and stairs would carry them. The tower had not been opened to anyone except workmen, but Cass noticed a ladder reaching up to a trapdoor and began to climb.

"Hey there, where are you going " called Woolworth.

"I'm going to see what's up here," returned Cass.

Mr. Woolworth, grown quite portly in his later years, was already out of breath from the unaccustomed exercise. But he would not be outdone.

"Just a minute, I'm coming with you," he called, huffing and puffing his way up the ladder. Once up the two walked around admiring the view, pleased as two schoolboys, and before they left they both wrote their names on the rafters.

Woolworth owned two pretentious homes, one on Fifth Avenue in New York, the other at Glen Cove, Long Island. After the latter one burned to the ground, he had built upon the site a palatial marble edifice of three stories which he named Winfield Hall, and in which he took up his permanent residence.

It seems sad that Jenny Creighton Woolworth, after having endured the hardships and poverty that she did while Frank was struggling for a place in the world, should not have been able to enjoy to the full the fruits of their efforts. Although she did have a few years of basking in the sunshine of luxury, her mind began to fade. In spite of the efforts of the best doctors, this condition increased until her mind was almost a complete

70

blank, and hired companions had to be with her at all times.

But in spite of her pitiable condition, she always was dressed in the height of fashion, and presided at the head of the table in the big dining room of Winfield Hall. Frank Woolworth lavished every luxury upon her that money could buy. Although she outlived her husband by almost five years, she never realized the fact.

On April 2, 1919, Mr. Woolworth, in spite of the glowing reports on the condition of his mercantile kingdom that he had received that day, was not feeling well physically and left his office early, not knowing that it was for the last time. The next day he worked with his secretary in his town house on Fifth Avenue, and the day after that he left for Winfield Hall for the weekend. By the time he reached there he was suffering great pain from a throat infection and high fever, and immediately took to his bed. For three days his doctors battled a combination of gall-stones, uremic and septic poisoning, and sore throat. All was in vain. The days of Frank Winfield Woolworth had run their course, and he passed away on April 8, 1919. In five more days he would have been sixty-seven years old.

The *New York Sun*, in its eulogy of Mr. Woolworth, seized upon the spirit of the ambition that had raised him to the very zenith of mercantile accomplishment, in a few succinct words:

"He gained fame by proving, not how little could be bought by much, but how much could be bought for little."

The billion dollar business complex that Mr. Woolworth started with a makeshift notions counter on the American Corner in Watertown had carried his name to the four corners of the earth. Today stores bearing the famous Diamond-W that became his trademark, can be found in many countries around the world; and these will continue to act as monuments to keep forever green the memory of a man who was, truly, a legend in his own time.

THE FOUR UNIQUES

Nearly every region has something that it can be proud of; something that, because of its unique qualities, can be boasted of with no fear of counter claims such as "something about like it," or perhaps "something just as good."

Superlatives cannot be applied to just any product or place or thing. In most cases they need to have withstood the test of time; the careful srutiny of the critical as well as the favorable observer. If an object or a product has passed this test and gone on for years on end, without an equal or even a close parallel, then indeed can it be called truly unique.

Many areas can claim one or more of these assets, but fortunate indeed, and very rare, is one which can claim four. But this seems to be the case with the Tug Hill region. Nothing ever has quite equalled the four examples here set forth, and probably never will.

* * * * *

The Tyler Coverlets

Although each in itself is a work of art, only one of the four examples mentioned, the Tyler coverlet, can sustain that boast when viewed from the artists's perspective. Its perfect symmetry of design and coloring, its evidence of the touch of the perfectionist, and the apparent quality of its construction, all testify to that fact.

Tyler coverlets were hand-woven from 1834 to 1858 by a family named Tyler, in a little village in Jefferson County, New York. The ancestors of Harry Tyler, the original designer and weaver of this product, had lived in Connecticut for many years, and were patriotically active in the Revolution. One of them had won the coveted Washington award for distinguished service.

Harry Tyler himself was born in Connecticut in 1801, but spent most of his boyhood in Millford, Otsego County, New York. Upon reaching maturity he married Ann Cole, and four healthy and intelligent children, Cynthia, Elman, Leman, and Leona, were born of this union.

In 1830 he moved to Boston, in Erie County, and two years later he bought a farm at North Adams, near Adams Center, and moved there. But he was not a farmer. His heart was not in the work, and he stayed there only one year.

His next move was to Butterville, a little hamlet two miles south of Smithville, in Jefferson County. Here he purchased a large house and seven acres of land, set out an orchard and established a large apiary. But these were only sidelines. For many years he had wanted to weave carpets and coverlets, and this he now decided to make his life work.

Being of an inventive nature, he designed and built his own looms, one for carpet and one for coverlets. These he set up in the large parlor of the house, with some of the machinery in the room above. And here were woven not only the first, but also the last, of the Tyler coverlets. The first of these came off the loom in 1834, the last twenty-four years later.

What started as a modest business soon burgeoned into a full time occupation for himself and his family. Mr. Tyler was a perfectionist, a man of high principle and a stickler for accurate detail; and the quality of his products was soon known far and near. His carpets looked and wore better than those of any other maker anywhere in the North Country. But it was for the bed

74

coverlets that he made that he soon became so justly famous.

These coverlets were woven of the finest materials, in the painstaking manner for which he was famous. The size was sufficient to cover a large double bed. Only two color combinations were used: red and white and blue and white. Woven in two-ply, the parts that were red or blue on one side were white on the other.

The dyes used by Mr. Tyler were all made from materials purchased from Elisha Camp. He used indigo for the blue, and for the brilliant red, cochineal, a substance made from the bodies of small female insects gathered from the cacti of Central America and Mexico. The thread was dyed in a huge brass kettle which was kept very clean and shiny by weekly scrubbing and polishing. This job fell to the two boys on each Saturday morning. No matter how good the fishing or hunting might be, no matter how packy the snow for snowball fights, this polishing job was the first order of the day, and must be attended to before anything else could be undertaken. No boots or shoes could be worn inside the kettle for fear of making scratches or blemishes on the surface. Whoever worked inside must do so in his bare feet.

It was also Elman's job to make deliveries of the finished products on horseback, and to pick up the dye materials. This latter task he liked best of all, as Mrs. Camp, a motherly woman, always had warm doughnuts or cookies for him.

Elman soon became the fastest weaver of the family. He could weave two half coverlets in two half days. The other halves of the two days he was allowed to go hunting. He was a good hunter, and an excellent shot.

No one outside the immediate family were ever allowed to work on a Tyler coverlet, and even they were never allowed to finish one alone, for fear that the secret of the process would escape. Harry Tyler himself always put the finishing touches on each one. When he died their manufacture stopped, because no one possessed the whole knowledge of how to produce one intact.

No two coverlets were ever made exactly alike in the design, which was composed of fruit, flowers, and vines. Each pattern was developed and drawn by the elder Tyler, with the exception of the eagle tradesman's mark, which was designed by son Elman. Harry, being of English extraction, liked the lion for a trademark, and used it for many years. It appeared woven into a lower corner of the coverlet, along with the year of manufacture, the name of the original owner, and the county to which it was to go.

Son Elman, who had become his father's right-hand man, one day brought up the subject of changing the trademark. He said that it seemed unrealistic to use a British trade-mark on an American product, and his father told him that if he wanted a change, he must draw the design. This Elman proceeded to do, and it consisted of an American eagle with wings outspread, a sheaf of arrows in one set of talons and olive branches in the other. From its beak floated a ribbon bearing the motto, "E Pluribus Unum." The elder Tyler approved it, and from that time on it was used.

Nearly every wealthy family in the North Country owned one or more Tyler coverlets, and most brides were given one or a pair at her "setting out" party. Each one had the owners' name woven in, but only two ever bore the name Tyler. One of these was made for a daughter, and the other was a wedding present for a daughter-in-law.

A handbill advertising the work of the Tyler family contained the following message:

"For coverlet and carpet weaving by H. Tyler, two miles south of Smithville, Jefferson County, N. Y. Persons wishing the above work done may be

76

assured that all work entrusted to my care will be done as well, if not better, than by any other weaver in the State. But in order to do this, the yarn must be prepared in the following manner."

There followed detailed instructions that would mean nothing to the present-day reader.

The cost of weaving one of these artistic masterpieces seems totally unrealistic today, but back then probably proved prohibitive to many who desired them. Using pre-dyed yarn furnished by the customer, the price was two and a half dollars, but if the yarn dyeing was included, that boosted the price to three dollars. This for a product of which many have survived well over a hundred years.

In 1843 Mrs. Tyler died, and after a respectful period of time, Harry married again. Another sizable family was born to this union. At the age of twenty years, Elman left home to learn the trade of carriage maker, and some time later, Leman did the same.

A little daughter by Harry Tyler's second marriage, whom he fairly worshipped, died in 1857. Upon returning home after the funeral in Smithville, Mr. Tyler suffered a stroke brought on by grief, people said. He died the next day at the age of fifty-seven, taking with him to the grave the secret of producing a Tyler coverlet in its entirety.

During the ensuing years the value of Mr. Tylers' masterpieces, never again equalled, have steadily increased. Now highly valued collector's items, it is very rarely that one is offered for sale. No one knows just how many were made. Many may be seen in the museums of historical societies. A few years ago a gentleman from California presented one to President Nixon, by whom it is very highly prized, and which now occupies an honored place in one of the guest rooms of the White House.

Burrville Cider

The other three uniques, although masterpieces in themselves, are better appreciated by the connoisseur of good things to eat and drink, than by the eye of the artist.

The author has always maintained that two of the very nicest things about autumn were crisp new apples and sweet cider, and certainly no cider ever made can surpass that pressed in the Burrville Cider Mill. It has been made each fall in the same locality for forty years, and always with the same painstaking attention to quality that has made it famous throughout the North Country. The owner, Homer Rebb, asserts that to his knowledge it has also gone to about fifteen other states.

The picturesque old building in which the mill is housed was first built in 1801 by Hart Massey for Raymond Burr, and the little settlement that grew up around it became known as Burr's Mills. This hamlet was the county seat of Jefferson County until 1807, when industrialists at Watertown harnessed Black River for water power, and the resulting upsurge of growth caused the seat of county government to be moved there.

The building was first used as a gristmill, and in later years as a sawmill, both water-powered, of course. During the ensuing decades the building became very run down, the dam went out, and the pen-stock that carried the water to the wheel fell apart. It was in a state of near collapse when it was purchased by Mr. Rebb, father of the present owner, in 1933.

In 1934 Mr. Rebb reset the waterwheel and rebuilt the pen-stock. He also repaired the building and re-arranged the equipment to require less labor. Water power continued to be used until 1945.

At first the cider-mill was rather crude, consisting of a wooden press and two hand-operated screws, also a large wooden tub. At that time the business was all custom pressing, with the customer bringing in the apples and receiving a gallon of cider for every sixteen pounds of fruit. What was left over was the property of the operator, and was sold for twenty-five cents a gallon. In connection with this the present owner comments:

"But in those days that quarter was all yours. There was no income tax, no workmen's compensation, and no social security to come out of it. And we didn't have to buy the apples. You could take the quarter to the store and buy three loaves of bread with it, and have a penny left over to mail a postcard."

The elder Mr. Rebb died in 1945, and the present owner inherited the business and immediately set about modernizing the plant. During the next few years stainless steel presses, tubing, and refrigerated storage vats were installed. A hydraulic press exerting many thousands of pounds pressure now does the actual work of pressing. A refrigeration unit was put into use whereby the apple juice is cooled within six minutes to just above the temperature of ice-water. This inhibits the growth of bacteria and preserves the fresh flavor of the product. A milk-plant standard of sanitation is observed at all times.

Early fall apples that are not thoroughly ripe are mellowed in a specially heated ripening room before they are used. All of the fruit is passed over a visual grader which turns each apple for inspection five or six times, and any showing rotten spots are taken out. A special straining system is used to filter out the settlings and impurities. In short, everything possible is done to insure the acme of quality for the product.

Mr. Rebb himself tests each run of juice. A former employee told the writer that he has been known to run from three to four hundred gallons down the drain because it did not meet with his rigid standard of approval. Also, all cider pressed one day must be sold by noon the next day. While this may appear to be a rather extravagant way to run a business, it does wonders in preserving the wonderful fresh flavor that keeps people coming back for more.

No deliveries are made by the plant. All the cider is picked up there, usually by individuals in one to five gallon lots. But a few distributors come with large tanks of up to a thousand gallons to be filled. It is then packaged in specially-printed two-quart containers for sale in retail outlets. And woe betide the distibutor who tampers with, dilutes, or in any way alters the purity of the product. Mr. Rebb is known to have banned one large distributor from his list of customers because he was selling another product labeled Burrville Cider.

The pressing season extends from mid-September until the second Sunday in November, and about fifty thousand gallons of juice are pressed each year. Mr. Rebb hires all local help, about thirty in all, and the annual payroll runs about twelve thousand dollars, which contributes substantially to the economy of the neighborhood.

Anyone who finds himself in the vicinity of Burrville during the cider season will do well to stop in at the Burrville cider mill. The welcome mat is always out, and a refrigerated container filled with some of the best cider to be found on the face of the earth awaits the pleasure of the thirsty visitor.

*   *   *   *   *

Heath Cheese

The old adage, "Build a better mousetrap and the world will beat a path to your door," still holds good; but not only for mousetraps. It also applies to cheese, as attested by the (figureatively speaking) hard-beaten track that leads right up to the door of the Sandy Creek Valley Cheese Factory, half way between Rodman and Whitesville, in Jefferson County.

80

For it is here that the famous Heath, or Rodman, cheese has been made continuously by the same family for sixty-five years. And during all that time there have been very few changes in the methods employed, and certainly never a let-up in the thoroughness and attention to detail that have made their cheese such a unique product.

It all began way back in 1909 when Orrin N. Heath, a young man born and raised in the area, rented a cheese-factory owned by Willis Kenfield and began making cheese there. Mr. Kenfield had built the factory on the bank of Big Sandy Creek in 1897, and had hired it run for him during the intervening years.

The first ancestors of Mr. Heath to enter the North Country had come to the Sandy Creek valley in 1805 as trappers. Taking a liking to the locality they settled near West Rodman, where they gradually evolved into farmers and tradesmen. At least one of them, Harrison Heath, had become a cheese-maker.

Orrin N. Heath was born at Toad Hollow, or West Rodman, in 1882, and as he grew up his fondness for, and proximity to, his Uncle Harrison instilled in him an interest in cheese-making that was to remain throughout the rest of his life. Even now, at ninety-one years of age, his dedication to the industry is unabated.

When he first rented the factory, Mr. Heath paid the owner a stated sum for each pound of cheese that he made; a sort of royalty as it were. In 1912 the building needed a new roof, and he went to Mr. Kenfield to see about having one put on. Mr. Kenfield refused flatly.

"Well, what are we going to do about it?" asked Mr. Heath. "I can't carry on business in a building with no roof, can I?"

"I'm going to sell the place to you," countered the owner.

"But how do you know I want to buy it?" asked Mr. Heath.

"Oh, you wan't to buy it, alright," said Kenfield confidently. "You want to keep on making cheese, don't you? So let's talk business."

So they talked business, with the result that Mr. Heath bought the factory, and he and his sons have made cheese there ever since.

In those days all the milk that the factory received was, of course, delivered by horse-drawn vehicles, and this limited the range of deliveries to farmers within a five or six-mile radius. But when automobiles began to come into common use, this of course increased the range, and at times between thirty and forty farmers were drawing their milk there. At that time an average of about three hundred and fifty thousand pounds of cheese were manufactured there yearly. Now only twelve farmers deliver milk there, but the yearly average runs about two hundred thousand pounds.

At the present time the business is run by two sons, Orrin W. and Malcomn Heath, who do all the work themselves. They claim that there is no secret to the excellence and unsurpassed flavor of their product. Like their father, they concentrate on making an old fashioned, washed curd cheese, which is naturally softer and more spongy and moist than conventional cheddar. "Made to be eaten up within six months," they say, and this seems to be true, as it is almost impossible to find Rodman cheese of even that ancient vintage.

During the past few years they have also manufactured a limited amount of pepper and garlic cheese, which has been about the only departure from the old fashioned methods initiated in 1909 by their father. This product has also attained such popularity that it is almost impossible to obtain.

Instead of modern and probably inferior chemical

82

substitutes, they still use old-fashioned rennet as a curdling agent in the milk. However, it is not now made at the plant as it used to be, but comes in two-gallon containers ready for use. It takes a very small portion of this liquid to curdle half a ton of milk.

Work at the plant starts at five o'clock in the morning. The first order of the day is to remove the cheese made the day before from the presses and place it on wooden storage shelves to dry. These cheeses are turned each day for three days to prevent the moisture from settling in one direction, and to obtain a dry rind. At the end of the three days required by law they are waxed, stamped with the date and place of manufacture, and placed in cold storage for a sixty-day waiting period before sale.

At about seven o'clock milk deliveries start coming in. The milk is strained into two large stainless steel vats. Rennet and lactic ferment, which imparts the flavor to the cheese, are added, and allowed to thicken. The coagulation is then cut into three-fourth-inch cubes by the use of a steel "comb," and is cooked at a precise heat until the curds and whey separate. The whey is then drawn off and the remaining cheese curd is cut into sections, washed, cooled, salted, and placed into hoops for pressing. The cheese is then bandaged, or dressed, and left under pressure until the next morning, during which time all the remaining whey is squeezed out.

The whey contains about three pounds of butter fat to one thousand pounds of liquid, or about equal to one hundred pounds of whole milk. Until lately it was run through a separator to remove this fat to be churned into butter. At one time the factory churned as high as fifty pounds of butter a day, and this constituted quite a sizable bonus profit. But in late years the amount of whey had diminished to a point where only ten pounds a day was realized, and the added fact that it was impossible to buy stainless steel parts for the steam turbine separator used for so many years rendered the practice impractical, and it was discontinued.

In the past, cheeses were made in a variety of weights. The largest was the forty pound size, followed by the "Twin," two cheeses of thirty-five pounds each in each box. Next was the tweny-five pound Daisy and another set of twins, two thirteen-pound picnics in a box. The five-pound Favorite and the three-pound Gem were the babies of the family. At one time a two-pound cheese was made, especially created for shipping to service men in World War II. Orrin W. had the hoops for these miniature delicacies made in Adams shortly after returning from service himself, in 1944. At present only forty-pound flats and three-pound picnics are made.

In 1910 the elder Mr. Heath exhibited some of his cheeses at the New York State Fair, and won a gold medal for excellency. But after the fair was over the officials reneged on their decision, declaring that there had been an error in the scoring and awarding the gold medal to another maker. Mr. Heath received the silver medal, which he still has; but, justifiably incensed, he vowed to never exhibit at the fair again.

In 1898 there were about thirteen hundred small country cheese factories in New York State turning out old fashioned cheese. But this number rapidly diminished during the first few decades of the nineteen hundreds, as large cheese-making companies infiltrated the rural areas, building huge plants and forcing many of the small operators out of business. Today there is only one other small factory besides Heath's doing business in the state. That one is at Russell, N. Y.

In spite of many chances to sell out to these large monopolies, Mr. Heath's dedication to cheese-making has caused him to continue in the face of all difficulties and competition. It has always been his policy to return

84

Number 22, first locomotive to see service on the Glenfield and Western Railroad. *(Photo courtesy Clarence Johnson)*

Engine No. 22 at rest. Engineer Charles Graves at left; fireman at right unidentified. *(Photo courtesy Charles Graves)*

Frank Bates, conductor; Mord Johnson, and a friend ride caboose of Glenfield and Western train. (*Photo courtesy Mrs. Frank Bates*)

All dolled up and going somewhere. (*Photo courtesy Mrs. Frank Bates*)

The Rock-cut in summer. (*Photo courtesy Mrs. Frank Bates*)

The Jitney, manned by Frank Bates and El-
don Wetmore, left to right. *(Photo courtesy
Mrs. Frank Bates)*

Number 75 built especially for use on the
Glenfield and Western Railroad. (Photo courtesy *Clarence Johnson)*

Number 75 took a nice long rest in a Tug Hill swamp. *(Photo courtesy Mrs. Frank Bates)*

Old 22 couldn't make up her mind . . . *(Photo courtesy Mrs. Frank Bates)*

Cleaning up the wreck at Bardo's Crossing.
(Photo courtesy Mrs. Frank Bates)

The wreck at Bardo's Crossing, cause of the
only fatality on the Glenfield and Western.
Caboose at left was crushed by logs in foreground, killing passenger. *(Photo courtesy
Mrs. Frank Bates)*

A steam-powered log loader placing logs on Glenfield and Western flat cars. *(Photo courtesy Charley Graves)*

The snowplow that ran away. *(Photo courtesy Mrs. Frank Bates)*

What they had to contend with in the Rock Cut. Superintendent Leslie Johnson standing on bridge. *(Photo courtesy Mrs. Frank Bates)*

Tough going on the crest of Tug Hill. *(Photo courtesy Mrs. Frank Bates)*

Clearing the tracks after a spring storm. Leslie Johnson, superintendent of the Glenfield and Western, standing on snow plow. *(Photo courtesy Mrs. Frank Bates)*

Snow . . . they had it. *(Photo courtesy Clarence Johnson)*

The demise of the old "Gee Whiz." Taking up rails in 1932. *(Photo courtesy Charles Graves)*

a goodly portion of his profits to the farmers in better milk prices, and his reputation for fair dealing has always insured him of a plentiful supply of milk. At times he has paid as much as a dollar a hundred more for milk than the large milk and cheese plants. During the years the efforts of himself and his two sons have evolved a product of such quality and flavor that the demand for it now far exceeds the output.

Mr. Heath has always been proud of the quality of his products, and ready to go to bat for them whenever the necessity arose. A rather amusing tale concerning this trait, as well as demonstrating the natural sagacity of the old gentleman, was related by one of the sons.

During the depression, when they were making more cheese than could be readily disposed of locally, Mr. Heath shipped some to a commission merchant in New York City for sale there. But he was very dissatisfied with both the returns from the sale and the reports on its disposal. The merchant stated that the product was of poor quality and sold very slowly, but Mr. Heath refused to believe this, especially the part about the poor quality.

"I think I'll go to New York and find out just what ails that cheese," he told his wife.

Supposedly he had figured out pretty closely just what course he meant to follow, for before starting out he printed a neat placard bearing his name and address, which he placed in the crown of the derby hat that he always wore in those days.

Arriving in New York he hunted up the merchant he had come the see, and introduced himself as a cheese wholesaler from Pennsylvania.

"I've come up to see if I can find a shipment of soft, creamy cheese of the best quality, such as my customers demand," he told the merchant.

"I have just what you want," the man replied. "A

shipment that I just got from upstate. Come with me and I'll show you." Whereupon he led Mr. Heath into a storage room and showed him the selfsame shipment of cheese that he himself had sent the man, and which was supposed to be of inferior quality.

Mr. Heath said that it looked good to him and asked the price, which turned out to be rather exorbitant.

"The price is rather steep," he told the merchant. "What makes it so high?"

"Quality," returned the merchant. "If you want real quality you have to pay for it."

"Well, I don't know," said Mr. Heath hesitantly. "Are you sure it's the highest quality?"

"Absolutely," returned the man. "You won't find any better anywhere."

This is what Mr. Heath had been waiting for. Taking off his derby he held it so that the man could read the placard inside.

"This is who I really am," he said.

To say that the man was nonplussed would be putting it mildly. Staring at the placard he realized that he had been totally outmaneuvered, outfoxed, and unhorsed. Slowly he stretched out his hand.

"I'm pleased to meet you, Mr. Heath," he said. "I can assure you that nothing like this will ever happen again." And the son declares that they sold the same man thousands of pounds of cheese after that, and always received top prices for it.

At present no shipments to commission merchants are necessary, as the demand at the factory far exceeds the supply. With the exception of the pepper and garlic cheeses, none are cut at the plant. Only whole cheeses are disposed of. Various distributors buy from the Heaths, but most of their product is sold to people within a radius of fifty miles, who like to visit the plant and talk with the friendly folks there.

The present owners say that their products have gone to every state in the Union, and at least one cheese was taken to France by a group of French cheese-makers who visited their factory. They have numerous scrapbooks filled with pictures and articles of and about them, of which they are justifiably proud. And all attest to the unique quality of Heath's Rodman cheese.

* * * * *

Croghan Bologna

Another unique product that has withstood the test of eighty years of constant manufacture in the same location and has earned for itself an enviable reputation for quality, purity, and gourmet flavor, is Croghan Bologna.

Manufactured in the village of Croghan, in Lewis County, it has been made continuously in the same building since 1894; and although Croghan has in the past enjoyed fame for many reasons, it is Croghan bologna that perpetuates its name throughout the state today.

In 1894 a Swiss immigrant named Fred Hunzicker came to the village and settled there. Being a butcher by trade, Herr Hunzicker opened a meat market on Main Street, and as a sideline started to manufacture a new and totally different type of smoked sausage, using a secret recipe brought with him from the old country. This product soon attracted the attention of the villagers, because of its appeallingly different flavor, and its fame continued to spread until it became known far and near as Croghan Bologna. Both the process and the name have been patented by the present operators.

Except for its general form, which vaguely resembles ring bologna, Croghan bologna has no resemblance to the conventional type. In the first place, it is made entirely of choice cuts of meat, not the left-over giblets and by-products after the expensive cuts have been utilized otherwise. And in flavor there is absolutely no comparison, the superior quality of the ingredients lending it a rich and robust, yet strangely delicate taste, unmatched by any other parellel product.

On February 16, 1921, Elmer Campany, who had formerly worked in another meat market in Croghan bought out Mr. Hunzicker's business, including the formula for the bologna. For twenty-nine years he and his sons, Anthony and John, continued to build up the business and add to the fame of their special products. In 1950 the elder Campany retired, and the meat market and bologna plant were purchased by the two sons, with Carl Nuspliger as a partner. Mr. Nuspliger sold out his interest to Anthony and John in 1963, and the two brothers incorporated under the name of The Croghan Meat Market, Incorporated.

During all this time the manufacture of the bologna went on unabated. Its reputation became more and more widespread, and soon the name became a household expression throughout the North Country. At first it took about two hundred pounds a week to supply the demand, but at present two thousand pounds or more are required each week.

The present owners have built up and modernized the plant into an efficient and smooth-running institution. All equipment that at some time or other during the manufacture of the bologna comes into contact with the ingredients has been converted to gleaming stainless steel. And everything is kept in an amazing state of cleanliness. Even the slaughter-house is spotless.

All of the meat ingredients of the product, which is primarily beef with a small percentage of other meats, are bought on the hoof. John Campany has charge of this department, attending cattle sales throughout the North

Country to secure their supply. Butchering is done in their own slaughter-house on one day of each week; and on this day, as well as on the two days of each week when they are making bologna, a United States Department of Agriculture inspector visits the plant to insure cleanliness and high quality.

After butchering, the carcasses are hung in a huge cooling room for a few days, or until all animal heat has been dissipated. Then they are taken into the cutting room where they are reduced to grinder-sized portions, and the big stainless steel grinder gobbles them down and spews them out as a finely ground mass. This in turn, is placed in a mixing machine along with the other ingredients, and thoroughly blended. The ingredients of the product are no secret, as the law requires them to be listed on each label. So it must be knowledge of proportions of each and blending know-how that produces the consistently fine flavor.

After blending, the mixture is placed in a stuffing machine and forced into prepared casings many feet long. The next step is to tie these casings into portions of from one and a half to three pounds each, after which they are cut apart and the ends are tied together in the form of rings.

From here the rings go to the smoke rooms, of which there are two, and hung up on racks near the ceiling. Slow fires of hard woods are lighted beneath them and they are smoke-cured to a just right color and flavor. No artificial smoke flavoring is used, only the real thing. Each smoke room is capable of curing a ton of bologna at a time.

Another delicious and totally different product, a smoked sausage of slightly larger than frankfurter size, is also produced in this plant. Made of the same fine ingredients, and manufactured under the same painstaking conditions as the bologna, this product has also

89

grown to be very popular, and about two hundred pounds are turned out each week. This process is also protected by patent rights.

Anthony Campany states that comparative prosperity in the business has always been good, even in depression times. He did say, however, that during those trying times, when jobs and money were so scarce, many times his father was asked by a customer to extend credit for a ring of bologna or a few pounds of meat. On many of these occasions, when he knew the customer to be especially deserving or especially unfortunate, Mr. Campany kindly forgot to set the sale down in his books, and such acts of big-heartedness endeared him to the memory of the townspeople.

The two Campany brothers and several trusted employees continue to carry out the business of turning out unique gourmet meat products which, once tasted, are never forgotten, and keep the customers coming back for more. And if that isn't success, then no one has ever attained it.

NELSON CLIFFORD,
INTREPID BEAR HUNTER

When we are young, the routine of day to day living seems to be tiresome and mundane, even boring at times. We live for the future, paying scant attention to the events and the people around us, accepting them as commonplace and uninteresting, except in a few cases. Now and then something or someone will impinge upon our consciousness as being a little special, a little out of the ordinary.

Viewed from a perspective of years, our former lives take on a rosy aura of romance that makes us realize how very fortunate we were. These were the good old days, we think. These were the good old happenings, the good old people. The events that stood out slightly become highlights. The people that impressed us more than usual gradually become heroes walking in seven-league boots. Fortunate indeed are those of us who have these things to cherish in our memories.

In the case of the author, this good fortune was many-fold, as I had many boyhood heroes. First, of course, was my own father, who knew everything and did everything right. And there were several others, among them Jack Dempsey, one of the great fighters of all time, and Babe Ruth, the Sultan of Swat, and my uncle Al Bush, one of the really great deer hunters because he thought and reasoned like a deer. There was Henry Ford, who made it possible for poor folks to own an automobile. And there was Mr. Clifford, whom I considered to be about the best rifle shot in the whole world.

91

Mr. Clifford was a tall, rangy gentleman already middle-aged when I first knew him. He and his wife, Julia, owned and, at that time operated, the famous old Cottrell Hotel in Greenborough, and my parents' farm adjoined theirs. About half a mile separated the two homes, so I had plenty of opportunity to become acquainted with the family.

His given name was Nelson, but nearly everyone called him "Nett." As I have mentioned, he was tall and rangy, all bone and muscle with hardly an ounce of fat. He had a long, flowing, grey mustache that often concealed a little grin; a grin that was, however, betrayed by the twinkle in his eye. His speech was very deliberate and about the softest in tone of any man's voice that I have ever heard.

Hard work and plenty of outdoor living had given Mr. Clifford an iron constitution that enabled him to hold his own with much younger men in the pursuit of outdoor sports and occupations. Even in his late sixties he possessed a deceptive walking gait that, in spite of its unhurried appearance, made most people hurry to keep up with him. And the keenness of his eye was never dulled to the extent where he had to take a back seat for anyone when it came to shooting a rifle.

Mr. Clifford was born at Port Ontario, New York, in 1863. While still a young man he came to the Boylston-Redfield area to engage in the lumbering occupation, and here he met and married Julia Brown. For the next few years the couple lived at several places in the vicinity, raising a family of four girls and four boys. During this time Mr. Clifford engaged in lumbering, farming, bear hunting, spruce gumming, trapping . . . anything to earn a living. Times were hard, but in those days families stood on their own feet and lived by their own efforts, rather than resort to welfare as too many do today.

In 1907 Mr. and Mrs. Clifford purchased the old

Cottrell Hotel in Greenborough. At this time the little settlement had started on its decline, but was still a going communiy. The hotel was a stop on the stage route between Rome and Watertown, and extra horses were kept in the big barn there. It was also a favorite stopping place for the drivers of the big cheese wagons that used to haul cheese from the north country to Rome, for shipment on the canal. This route was, of course, the Old Military Road from Rome to Sackets Harbor, built in 1814 for the transport of military supplies between the two places.

My own first memory of Mr. Clifford began when I was about four years old. At that time he was doing a lot of bear hunting. Bears were very plentiful, in fact they were much too plentiful to please the farmers who raised sheep. There was no law protecting them, and they were hunted indiscriminately at any season of the year. A favorite time for hunting them was in early spring when the females came out of their dens, bringing with them one or two cubs born in hibernation. These little fellows could not travel fast or for long distances, and a hunter discovering their tracks in the snow could be assured of not having to follow them far. When close-pressed the mother would force them to climb a tree, while she went on in an endeavor to draw the hunter away from her offspring. Coming upon the tree, the hunter would then tie a jacket or bransack around the trunk, knowing that the cubs would not climb down over anything containing human scent.

He would then go on until he overtook and killed the female for her hide, and on his way back would cut down the tree containing the babies and capture them alive. These were sold to a dealer named Turner who made periodic visits to the area for the purpose. Mr. Clifford sold to him, but between visits the surplus built up in prime hunting seasons. These were kept in a small outbuilding at the back of the hotel, running loose in a room of which the floor was covered deep with sawdust.

One day the old gentleman took me by the hand and led me out to see the cubs. He had twenty-four of them at that time, and they were quite an unforgettable sight for a four-year-old. Going in among them he selected one and brought it out for me to play with. This one was as tame and gentle as a kitten, and made a nice plaything; but there were some among the number who displayed a streak of mean temper. These would snarl and snap their little teeth, and strike with their tiny forepaws, whenever he extended a hand toward them. Needless to say, the sight impressed me in a manner which I will never forget.

As I grew older my interest in all kinds of hunting and fishing grew greater. A good trout stream ran down across our land and near the old hotel, and I also acquired an old twenty-two rifle with which I hunted woodchucks on the meadows and side hills on my parents' and Cliffords' farms. Whenever possible I would stop and talk with Mr. Clifford, or just listen to him talk. It was on one of these excursions that I witnessed a demonstration of marksmanship that I never forgot.

It happened that unexpected company arrived at the Clifford's right after I did. Of course they were invited to stay to dinner, and they gladly accepted. As was usual on farms in those days, a chicken dinner could always be relied upon for quick and easy accessibility, so Mrs. Clifford came out to where the men were talking (and I was eagerly listening) in front of the barn.

"Nett, I wish you'd kill a couple of hens for dinner," she requested.

Mr. Clifford stepped into the barn and came out shortly with his 38-55 Winchester and a small dish of corn, the contents of which he scattered on the ground. Immediately he was almost deluged by hens that came

94

running from all directions to join the writhing mass, all trying to get at the feed.

"Now Jule, show me which ones you want," he said.

Mrs. Clifford pointed out the two fat hens that she wanted, and her husband nodded his head. Up came the rifle, following the movements of one of the luckless birds. When the time was just right, the gun exploded and the hen flopped in the dust minus her head. In a very few moments the other suffered the same fate, and none of the rest of the milling throng suffered the slightest harm.

Now this didn't surprise me greatly, but the dinner guest, who wasn't familiar with his host's prowess with firearms, was utterly flabbergasted, and his eyes were round with astonishment.

Another example of this man's shooting ability was witnessed by the author some years later, after he had graduated to deer hunting status. A party of eight or ten hunters, including Mr. Clifford, my dad, and myself, were hunting in the Mad River section, and had come together at noon to eat our lunches. After the sandwiches had all been consumed we sat about in the warm autumn sun idly talking, some enjoying pipes or cigarettes, with the appearance of a deer about the farthest possible thing from our minds.

And it was just at this time that one did choose to appear. It was a medium-sized buck that tried to sneak past us, and he had half-way done so before anyone noticed him. Of course everyone grabbed for his rifle and started shooting, and after the first shot had sounded that deer was transformed into a living rocket. Now, there were some very good marksmen among that group, but in the general confusion nobody touched a hair, and the shooting quickly diminished as one by one the guns went empty.

All this time Mr. Clifford had sat calmly smoking

his pipe and had not taken up his rifle. Now, however, he came to life and picked up the old 38-55.

"Well boys, I guess he's going to get away from us after all," he said in his slow, soft voice. By the time he had leveled the rifle the buck was nothing but a fast disappearing white tail, but when the shot rang out the white tail went down and the deer faltered, staggered a few leaps, and pitched forward to the ground.

Now the author knows this to be true because he saw it himself. Mr. Clifford never bragged about his shooting . . . he let it speak for itself.

It was as a bear hunter that Mr. Clifford really shone, however. He and the author's grandfather, who was also a good bear hunter, used to banteringly call one another "The Old Bear Hog." An article in the June 29, 1916, issue of the *Sandy Creek News* stated, "Nelson Clifford of Redfield has shot or trapped over two hundred black bears in that section." By this late date the bear population was on the wane in that area, but it is safe to say that he killed several more after that. This was quite an enviable record, to say the least.

If all the bear hunting experiences undergone by Mr. Clifford could be chronicled, they would make up a large and interesting book. Although the black bear is not by nature a ferocious or aggressive creature, and one that will avoid contact with humans whenever possible, he can still, when wounded or cornered, become a very dangerous antagonist. Especially is this true of a female with small cubs. It seems impossible that anyone with the magnitude of experience enjoyed by Mr. Clifford could have escaped having at least a few dangerous confrontations with his quarry. Unfortunately, he was not a man to boast of his exploits, so most of them were never known. He often said jokingly that his biggest scare came from a dead bear instead of a live one.

It seems that one day he had been tracking a large

96

bear for some distance, but the animal had sensed that it was being followed and had taken refuge in a large hollow log. Coming upon the scene, the hunter had at first tried smoking the bear out, but the wind was not in the right direction to drive the smoke into the cavity, so the effort failed.

Not to be thwarted so easily, Mr. Clifford fired a couple of shots into the opening in the log. Immediately thereafter there was a flurry of snarling and scrambling inside the log, but nothing came out. Eventually the noise subsided, to be replaced by an ominous silence. The hunter was quite sure that the game was dead, but in a case such as this, almost sure was not good enough. The only way to get the animal out was to crawl in there and pull him out, and to face a possibly wounded beast did not appeal to Mr. Clifford at all.

But he knew that this was the only possible way, so he made his preparations. Taking his hatchet he cut a sturdy pole about six feet long. He knew that it would be impossible to use his rifle in the narrow confines of the log, and neither would he have room to wield his hatchet. This left only his hunting knife as a weapon, so with this in one hand and the pole pushed ahead of him with the other, he gingerly crawled into the opening.

Some time had now elapsed, and as is often the case, considerable gas had collected in the chest and abdominal cavities of the deceased animal. As the hunter inched his way forward, the end of the extended pole suddenly made contact with the beast's side, and it responded with a grunt caused by escaping gas. To Mr. Clifford it sounded like a snarl, and his heart fairly blocked his throat as he mentally pictured himself trying to fend off a wounded bear with only a knife.

But nothing more happened, so after a while he poked again. Another grunt came out of the darkness; nothing else. After repeated pokes brought the same re-

97

sponse, he decided that the bear must be dead, so he continued his slow advance. After a while his hand encountered a furry paw, and as no gnashing teeth greeted him, he grasped it and started to tug backwards. It took quite a while and a great deal of energy to get that bear out of the log, but he finally accomplished it.

"He couldn't of bit me anyway," Mr. Clifford said afterward. "He was headed in the wrong direction."

Mr. Clifford possessed a dry sense of humor, and liked to play a practical joke now and then. A comical little episode illustrating this trait was related to me by the late Charles Williams, whom I first knew as a rural mail carrier but who years before that taught school in the rural districts of Boylston and Redfield. Mr. Williams also had a sense of humor, even when the joke was on him.

At the time of which he spoke, he was teaching in the little one-room school in what was known as the Button District. As was the custom, he boarded with a family in the district, in this instance with the Cliffords. The following tale is as nearly like he told it as I can remember.

"Nett was planning a two-day trip after spruce gum," Mr. Williams related. "He was going in to his camp on Friday, and I wanted to go with him to hunt hedgehogs (porcupines) so I closed school for that day and went along. We started way before daylight, planning to pick gum that day and spend the night in Nett's camp away up in the green timber. One of the older Clifford boys, I can't remember which, was going in to the camp that day and have it all warmed up for us.

"Of course we used snowshoes . . . the snow was five feet deep. Along in the afternoon those shoes were getting to be a little heavy, and I didn't have the faintest idea which way it was to camp. The way we had been circling

98

and wandering to find gum, I began to wonder if Nett did either. So I asked him.

" 'Well, I think I do,' " Nett answered, looking around him kind of uncertain like.

"We kept on going, and pretty soon it began to snow. The snow kept getting heavier, and I kept getting more nervous. It also started getting dark, and the darker it got the more certain I was that we were lost.

" 'Don't you think we'd better holler for help?' " I asked Nett.

" 'Oh, I don't think it's necessary,' said Nett, 'not just yet anyway.'

"Well, the snow kept coming down harder and harder. Soon it was impossible to see two rods in any direction. But Nett kept right on going, with me trying to keep up. All at once he stopped and stood looking around with a puzzled look on his face.

" 'How'd you like to camp right here for the night?' he asked.

"I told him that I wouldn't enjoy it at all, and he said,

" 'A while back you wanted to holler for help, and I think right now is the time to do it. Go ahead and holler.'

"I didn't need any more urging, and let a whoop out of me that they must have heard in Lowville. And right there, not fifty feet away, a door opened and lantern light came pouring out. Nett had brought us right to camp in spite of the storm and darkness, but he sure had me scared for a while. I really shouldn't have been, though, because he was like an Indian in the woods."

In 1926 the state decided to erect a fire observation tower on Caster Hill, up near Mad River. The site chosen was on land owned by Mr. Clifford, and leased from him for that purpose. He had a small camp near the tower, and was hired as the first observer to serve there. Although he was then well along in years, his eyesight was still keen enough to detect a slight smoke haze away up on the heights of Tug Hill. He served as observer until 1931, when the position was taken over by a son-in-law, Mellvin Clemons.

During the 1920's the Clifford family suffered tragedy when one of their younger sons met an untimely death beneath the wheels of a railroad train. Then, in 1929, Mrs. Clifford passed away, and after that the old gentleman became lonely and restless. He was a frequent visitor at our home, but he spent more and more time in his camp on Caster Hill. In 1937 he died peacefully in his sleep in the old Cottrell Hotel, which was no longer operated as a hostelry and was occupied by his youngest daughter and her husband, Mr. and Mrs. William Hasseler.

Thus passed into history a truly great woodsman, a bear hunter without a peer, and a highly respected gentleman of the old school; and also, one of my own boyhood heroes.

EARLY LIFE ON TUG HILL

Henry H. Lyman was born and grew up among the hills and gulfs of Lorraine township, on the northwest flank of Tug Hill, back in the days when the country was really wild and primitive. His boyhood occurred in pre-Civil War days, and recollections of it were related in after years in a delightful book that is the finest description of rural life in those bygone days that this writer has ever come across.

In it, Mr. Lyman not only related the story of day-to-day living, but also the manner in which he learned some of the moral lessons that helped him to become in later years the upstanding and solid citizen that he was.

Mr. Lyman's ancestors came to Lorraine from the New England States in the very early eighteen-hundreds, bringing all their possessions on a "stone-boat," or sledge, drawn by a team of oxen. This was even before the establishment of the "Old State Road," which was cut through the virgin forest in 1814 from Fort Stanwix at Rome to the naval base at Sackets Harbor.

The State Road was deemed necessary rather than rely on water transportation, after the British fleet on Lake Ontario blockaded an American flotilla of scows loaded with naval supplies at the mouth of Sandy Creek; the ambush and battle there, in which the British lost heavily; and the subsequent carrying of the huge cable destined for use on a warship being built at Sacketts Harbor. This big rope was seven inches in diameter and thirty-six rods (five hundred ninety-four feet) long, and weighed "ninety-six hundred-weight, three quarters and twenty-six pounds" (from an old diary kept by one of

Mr. Lyman's ancestors). It was carried overland from Sandy Creek to Sackets Harbor on the shoulders of patriots gathered for the purpose. Eighty-six men working as a team and carrying an approximate one hundred twenty-eight pounds each, transported it for a distance of three miles; then another eighty-six relieved them for the next three miles. In this way it reached its destination and many a man wore the scars engendered by the grueling task for years to come.

There were no roads through the area when Mr. Lymans' ancestors arrived. The woods were thick and the terrain was rocky, no place for a wheeled vehicle. But with the stoneboat they could dodge the boulders and fallen logs, and in this way they finally made their way to a location about two miles south of the village of Lorraine, or, as it was later nicknamed, The Huddle.

Here they settled on the banks of an exuberant little stream that gave promise of plenty of water power. During the ensuing years a large farm was cleared and established, with a huge, rambling farmhouse that became known as "The Old Homestead," and which still stands. And here Henry H. Lyman was born and grew to manhood, amidst scenes of intense industry and adventures that produced many interesting and amusing anecdotes.

Henry's father was a very ambitious and enterprising man, and had many other irons in the fire besides the operation of the farm. For instance, he owned a series of sawmills over the years that specialized in "custom sawing," in other words, he took other people's logs and sawed them into lumber for half of the finished product. This lumber was then sold or traded for other merchandise, as was then the custom. Very little money ever changed hands. Most of these old mills had the up-and-down-type saw; but the last one he ever owned had a circular saw, an innovation in those days.

Contiguous to the mill was a cooper-shop, in which

he made all the tubs, buckets, barrels, and storage vats used around the farm, and some for sale. Most of this work was done at night, after the regular day's work was finished, and in it young Henry had to help. Usually his duties consisted of holding the lantern for light, and handing his father the various tools as they were called for. And it was in connection with this work that he learned a very important lesson.

Like very many persons before and since, he had somehow developed the habit of answering "Hey?" whenever spoken to, even though he had clearly understood what the person had said. This became very annoying to the boy's father, who did not believe in wasting anything, even words.

One evening they were at work in the cooper shop, with Henry sleepy as usual, and the father asked the boy to hand him some tool that he needed. Also, as usual, Henry responded with the familiar "Hey?" even though he had heard perfectly. The father laid down his tools and turned to face the boy.

"Henry," he said, "you heard what I said. Don't let me hear you use that word 'Hey' again."

They resumed their work, Henry becoming more and more sleepy. Presently the father said, "Hand me the crooked frow," and true to habit, the boy responded "Hey?" This time the father did not waste words. Instead, his big open hand hit the boy a resounding slap beside the face that toppled him from his stool and landed him among the shavings on the floor.

Henry was dumbfounded. Never before had his father hit him. But even though not a word was spoken by either one, he knew quite well the reason for the slap, and accepted the fact at its face value. And it was a lesson that he never forgot for the remainder of his life.

Discipline was harsh in those days. But it produced

real men, vastly different from the all-too-frequent non-conformists who are the products of present-day parental permissiveness.

Another pursuit engaged in by the elder Lyman was the operation of an ashery. Wood ashes were bought from surrounding farmers for from ten to twelve cents a bushel for house ashes, and five to seven cents a bushel for field ashes; and after having been subjected to a rather complicated system of refinement, were converted into potash and pearl ash. These products were then transported overland to Rome, where they were loaded onto boats. Potash sold for eighty dollars a ton delivered, and was one of the few products that could be turned into ready, actual cash.

This money was then converted into merchandise for the store that he conducted in conjunction with the other businesses. The store stocked most of the commodities required by the surrounding country folks, and the goods were usually paid for in ashes; thus completing not a vicious, but a very fortunate circle. Without it, many an old settler would have found it very difficult to carry on.

Another later enterprise engaged in was the operation of a shingle mill. This did not prove to be a big success, due to the proximity of Redfield, only eighteen miles away, where a very superior type of shaved spruce shingle was made. It was said that nearly every home in Redfield was at that time a shingle factory, and their product completely outshone the sawed hemlock-type produced by the mill. So, with such stiff competition, the shingle mill saw very little use as such, and was soon converted to other purposes.

With so much activity going on all around them, Henry and his brother and three sisters learned early in life the lessons of industry and thrift that served them so well in later years. Each had his or her own duties to perform, and they did them with very little urging or complaint.

The mother had charge of making the butter and cheese, as well as the cooking, baking, and other household duties; and in all these she was ably assisted by the girls in the family. In addition, they spun, wove, or knit most of the clothing worn by the family. Very few "store bought" garments were ever indulged in. Another duty left to them in springtime sugaring season was the "final boil" of the various maple products. This was accomplished in a big copper kettle swung into the huge fireplace in the cooper shop, and they knew just when to suspend the boiling operation in order to make syrup, or soft sugar to be stored in earthen crocks, or the fine-grained hard sugar to be molded into cakes and sold to customers of the store.

Helping with the sugaring was one of Henry's favorite duties, and, incidentally, one that taught him another of life's most valuable lessons.

This operation began in late winter, as soon as the freezing nights and warm sunny days started the sap coursing up from the roots of maple trees toward the twigs and branches that would later bear the leaves. Usually there were still many feet of snow on the ground, and this greatly hindered the work of tapping the trees and hanging the wooden buckets. Only the hard or sugar maples were tapped, the sap of the soft maples being flat and tasteless.

Often snowshoes had to be used in gathering the sap, which was carried in pails to the nearest gathering roads, where it was dumped into a huge wooden gathering vat on a sleigh drawn by a pair of gentle and patient horses. It was then transported to the sugar house, in which was an arch built of flat stones mortared together with blue clay from a nearby creek bed. On this had been placed three large iron pans, each about four feet square, and into these the sap was ladled and the boiling began. Once started, the boiling went on day and night until either the supply of sap or the sugaring season was exhausted.

It was this boiling operation that Henry really loved, especially the night boiling. The wood for fuel had been cut and stacked against the sugar-house the summer before, so there was little reason to go far outside. Usually one or more neighbor boys would spend the night with him, and the time not actually consumed in stoking the fires or watching the pans was spent in playing games or bantering conversation. Often the boys would stand in the open doorway and peer out into the dark forest, and what had been familiar scenes in daylight would be transformed into strange and mysterious lands peopled by who knew what. Sometimes the hooting of an inquisitive owl or the lonely barking of a fox would start the cold chills coursing up their spines. But once back inside with the door shut, and the flickering lantern furnishing light, the night with all its mysteries seemed to be shut out, and a sense of cozy security reigned within.

Always there was a milkpail full of lunch, and often they brought along eggs which they cooked in the boiling sap, the flavor of which penetrated the shells and imparted to the eggs a distinctive taste never encountered anywhere else.

There was also a makeshift bunk in the sugarhouse where they could take turns catching a little sleep as the night progressed. But never would they allow anything to wholly divert their minds from the real business at hand; that of keeping watch of the syrup pans. The boiling sap was capricious and had to be closely watched. Sometimes for no apparent reason it would foam up and spill over the sides of the pan, and it was then brought back to its normal level by either adding a little cold sap, or tossing in a small cube of salt pork or tallow. As the consistency of the boiling mixture became progressively thicker, it was transferred from one pan to the next. After the third it was placed in tubs and taken to the cooper shop for the final "syruping off" by Henry's mother and sisters.

As one can readily see, this imposed a lot of responsibility on the operator, especially on a lad the age of Henry. But he was always worthy of the trust — except once. And it was then that he learned a very big lesson.

On this particular occasion things had gone well until about daylight, when Henry developed an overwhelming curiosity to see how things were going at a neighboring sugar-house about half a mile away. When he made known to a cousin who had spent the night with him, his intention of visiting the place, the cousin voiced a protest.

"I dont' think we'd aughten to go, Henry," he said. "Somethin' might go wrong and your pa'd be awful mad."

But Henry was determined, and no argument would change his mind.

"But what could go wrong?" he scoffed. "We'll bank the fires up good, and we won't be gone more'n half, three-quarters of an hour. No one will ever know."

The cousin saw that it would do no good to argue, so they banked the fires and took off on a dog-trot for the other sugar-house. After chatting for a few minutes, they started back home, but had not gone far when they became aware of the heavy smell of burning sugar adrift on the morning air. Sprinting the rest of the way, they burst into their sugar house to find the number three pan, the one containing the heavy mixture, all afire and containing only a black, reeking sludge. What would have provided ten gallons of top grade syrup, at seventy-five cents a gallon, had been totally destroyed.

The boys were now in a quandary. Henry knew that his father would be very angry if he found out that the boys had deserted their post; not so much for the loss of

107

the syrup as for their dereliction of duty. He decided to keep him from finding out if possible.

As soon as the pan had cooled enough, they set desperately to work, scraping and scouring to remove the black, scaly residue from the burned pan. When this had been done they reset the pan and filled it from the other pans. The burned debris was buried deep in the ash heap, and when Henry's father arrived about eight o'clock, the boys were busily tending the fires. The older man sniffed suspiciously.

"Seems to me I smell burnt syrup," he commented.

"The pan boiled over," answered Henry, busily poking away at the fire. His cousin gave him a surprised and aggrieved look, but he said nothing and Henry paid him no mind.

"Why didn't you throw in a piece of pork?" queried the father.

"It is all used up," answered Henry. He had made sure that this was true by dumping it all in the fire.

"You should have dumped in some cold sap," Henry's father said.

"I did," lied Henry. "But it didn't do any good."

The father said no more about the matter at the time, but now and then he shook his head as though puzzled. Henry went home to eat breakfast and snatch a few hours sleep, but the realization of what he had done bothered his conscience to the extent of ruining both his appetite and his sleep. He knew that he had done an abominable thing, but he did not have the courage to confess and face the music.

His father did not mention the incident again; but the next day his mother said to him, "Henry, whatever happened to that one batch of syrup?"

"I don't know," answered Henry, glibly telling another lie to cover up those already told.

108

"Well, I never saw syrup with so many settlings in it," said his mother.

Both Henry and his disapproving cousin kept the secret for many years. From it he learned the valuable lesson that the betrayal of a trust was an unforgivable thing, and that the telling of an untruth to cover it up was even more reprehensible. And always after that, whenever he would observe a person desperately telling one lie to cover up another, he would comment,

"I guess that fellow must have burnt his syrup."

In early spring, green things began to make their appearances in field and woods. Cowslips poked their bright green leaves and yellow blossoms out of marshy spots, and were eagerly picked, cooked with salt pork, and relished by appetites jaded by weeks of winter fare. Horseradish was dug, the roots washed and ground fine, and diluted with a little vinegar served as a breath-taking (actually) pick-me-up for many other kinds of food. The tender, war-club curled shoots of the common hog-brake were cooked and served with a milk sauce that made them taste very much like asparagus. And in the woodlands, wild leeks pierced the brown leaf mold with their tightly rolled leaves, which soon spread and perfumed the air with their pungent aroma. These were also welcomed by the country folk, who ate the onion-like bulbs raw or cooked the whole plant as greens.

The advent of leeks had one serious drawback however; for cattle roaming the woodland pastures also had an eye out for the first green shoots to appear, and relished them quite as much as humans. Eaten by the cattle, they imparted a very rank and disagreeable flavor to the milk and butter.

To counteract this, a raw leek was placed on each plate at mealtime, to be eaten before any other food was partaken of. This served to offset the rancid, unpleasant

109

taste, even if it did keep the eaters' breath foul and unbearable for days on end.

As the season progressed, one farm chore followed another in never-ending procession. Fences broken down by the weight of winter snows had to be mended and new rails put in where necessary. Plowing that had not been done the preceding fall had to be caught up. Stones had to be picked from the newly-plowed ground each spring. Then followed endless days of walking behind a team dragging a peg-tooth harrow. This was a tedious and dusty job, but one that must be done to prepare the somewhat stony soil for planting.

Oats and corn were the principal fodder crops, and were planted as soon as the ground could be prepared. Potatoes were planted during the full moon in June, which was the traditional potato planting time in the North Country.

Between the planting and the hoeing and cultivating would usually come a couple of weeks that could be devoted to catching up odd jobs that had no special place in the calendar. It was then that the mill-race was cleaned and repaired, roofs patched if needed, stone walls repaired or new ones built. The sugar house received a going over, the arch newly mortared, and wood cut for the next sugar season.

It was also usually during this time that the road or poll tax was "worked out." The local path-master had a list on which were the amounts assessed against each land owner for the upkeep of the roads, and these assessments were paid off by labor on the highways; so much a day for each man or grown boy, so much a day for a team and wagon.

These periods were generally greatly enjoyed by the participants, as it was then that all the local gossip, political issues, et cetera, were thoroughly discussed, stories and anecdotes exchanged and, especialy among the younger element, feats of strength and agility were bragged about and demonstrated. It was a time for socializing and relaxation, in spite of the vast amounts of hard labor performed; and it kept the roads in passable condition at very little monetary cost to the people.

When the corn and potatoes had reached a height of three or four inches, cultivating and hoeing began. The former was accomplished by the use of a hand cultivator drawn by one horse that was usually led by a small boy or girl to keep him between the rows. Sometimes the tediousness of this leading job was alleviated by the leader being allowed to ride astride the horse's back, hanging to the hames and steering by the reins, or lines. This was somewhat better, as it allowed a fellow a chance to scan the imaginary plains for buffalo or Indians, and to pick off an imaginary redskin or two with well-placed shots from an imaginary rifle. But it did not pay to let one's imagination wander too far, or an unimaginative mount might wander off crosslots, dragging the cultivator and a cursing parent or hired man behind.

Occasionally someone owned a horse smart enough to keep between the rows by itself, and such a horse was really treasured, as the leading chore was universally detested by the young folks.

Inversely, corn hoeing was a chore that Henry loved, mainly because it was a group activity participated in by all the male inhabitants of the farm. It was backbreaking work, but the close proximity of the workers to one another permitted a great deal of conversation and good-natured chaffing that proved to be lots of fun. Indirectly, it was the cause of his learning another of life's basic truths.

One of his greatly admired boyhood heroes was the husband of an older sister; a stalwart, robust young fellow whom the boy tried to emulate in every way. Habitually this young man would go about from spring to

111

fall wearing a coat of tan that would have done credit to an Indian, and with sleeves rolled up to his shoulders, displaying bulging muscles in forearms and shoulders. This display greatly impressed Henry, especially the deep, chestnut tan. What he did not realize was that it had not been acquired in a day, but had come from daily exposure to a strengthening sun during long weeks of outdoor labor.

So the first year that Henry was old enough to help with the corn hoeing, he decided to duplicate in a day or so what it had taken his brother-in-law weeks to accomplish. Bravely rolling his sleeves up high and unbuttoning the front of his shirt, he took his place beside his hero in the line of hoe-wielding laborers, exposing to the now potent sun arms and chest pale and tender from long weeks of protection.

By noon these areas of tender skin had assumed a deep pink color, and by mid-afternoon had become a painful, angry red. Henry gritted his teeth and toiled bravely on. "No smart, no tan," he reasoned. But by suppertime he was in real agony, and a deep fever wracked his whole body. He spent a sleepless night, during which his mother tried to alleviate his suffering by applications of cold vinegar and packs wet with a strong tea solution.

There followed two days of recovery in bed, during which he had time to reflect upon his mistake. Then came several days of itching, burning recuperation while the sun-blistered skin peeled away in large patches, leaving painful sores that healed slowly. By the time he was fully recovered, he had learned a never-to-be-forgotten fact of life: that good things come slowly and can seldom be hurried, and that no amount of pretense, sham, or emulation can take the place of good old-fashioned experience.

The potatoes were usually weeded and hoed twice before the "hilling up" operation began. This took place when the plants were about a foot high, just before the blossoms appeared. Right after the last cultivating, a special shovel-plow was run through the rows, shoving the fresh soil into high-shouldered ridges on both sides of the plants. This served a double purpose; it provided cover to prevent sunburn for the uppermost potatoes, and it did away with the necessity for the tuber-bearing roots having to burrow deep to find room to expand. Thus the potatoes actually grew above ground level, and made their digging much easier in the fall.

Another task connected with potato growing that was especially distasteful to Henry was the "bugging," or ridding the plants of the Colorado beetle, better known as the potato bug. This had to be done several times each summer. The adult beetle was about the size of a pea, hard-shelled, with yellow and black striped wing covers that gave it a rather racy appearance. Each female laid thousands of eggs on the underside of the potato leaves, easy to detect because of their bright yellow color. The heat of the sun soon hatched these eggs into small, brick-red slugs, whose voracious appetites soon transformed into *large* brick-red slugs, and the host plant into a leafless skeleton. When they had reached a size almost as large as the parents, they burrowed into the soil, only to emerge in a few days as hard-shelled adults, ready to start the vicious cycle all over again.

These insects had no natural enemies. No animal or bird would eat them because of their obnoxious taste, so it was strictly up to the farmer to rid himself of the pests. This could be, and sometimes was, done by poisoning. Paris Green or arsenate of lead was mixed with sifted wood ashes and placed in a porous bransack, which was given a vigorous shake over each potato hill. A puff of poison-laden ashes would emerge and settle on the foliage of the potato plant, which, if eaten by the bugs, would cause their death. This was usually done early in

113

the morning, when the mixture would cling to the dew-moistened leaves.

But this system had several drawbacks. The poison cost money, of which there was very little, and a sudden shower could wash it all away. Then there was always the chance of domestic animals, or even people themselves, becoming affected by the poison. And the eggs on the under side of the leaves were not eliminated. It was a messy and uncertain method, so usually the old reliable "stick and pan" system was resorted to.

This method was vastly more gratifying to the thrifty farmers, in that it cost nothing and could be done by small boys or girls. All the equipment needed was an old pan or wide-mouthed pail, and a stout paddle about two feet long. The operator simply held the pan at one side of the plant, lopped the foliage over it with the paddle, and gave the plant a few hard shakes. Most of the bugs would fall into the receptacle. The bright yellow egg clumps were picked off and joined the bugs in the pan. Every now and then the pan was given a good shake to dislodge the bugs that tried to escape by crawling up the sides.

When the pan was partly filled it was taken to the house, if not too far distant, and boiling water was poured over the contents. If the potatoes were far afield, a little kerosene was poured into the pan and mixed thoroughly. This killed most of the bugs, which were then dumped upon the ground, a match applied, and the whole stinking mess went up in a cloud of evil-smelling smoke.

This job could become very monotonous and distasteful to a small boy, especially if the sun was hot and the potato field several acres in extent. But it was a job that had to be done, one of the inescapable facts of life, and its acceptance helped to prepare him for the many other larger problems that he would encounter in later life.

114

Time was, and within the memory of Henry's father, when this pest was unknown in the North Country. Potatoes could and did grow in unhindered proliferation. Then suddenly one day folks who lived along the shores of Lake Ontario found the beaches littered with windrows of these strange looking, drowned beetles. It was supposed that a vast flight of them, originating no one knew where, had been plunged into the lake and perished.

But, unfortunately, not all of these bugs were dead. Many of them quickly dried out and, spreading their wings, flew away inland, where they quickly gravitated to potato fields. At first they were considered a novelty, no one realizing that here was one of the most deadly enemies of potatoes known to man. Farmers quickly came to understand this, however, but before they learned to control the pests, many potato crops had been ruined.

The infestation was not confined to New York State alone, but quickly spread over the whole eastern section of the nation. Today, with all sorts of insecticides and scientific methods readily available, these pests are easily controlled.

Haying was another task that entailed a great deal of grueling manual labor. In Henry's boyhood the entire operation was accomplished by man-power. The mowing was done with scythes, and continued to be until along in 1818, when a man by the name of J. I. Case, of Williamstown, New York, perfected the first horse-drawn mowing machine. Even then, these machines could be afforded only by the well-to-do. Raking and "bunching up" was done with wooden hand-rakes, and the sun-dried hay was pitched onto and off from the hay wagons by men and boys wielding pitch-forks. The scatterings were cleaned up behind the loaders by small boys and girls with wooden hand-rakes.

In late summer the grain was harvested by the use of "cradles," a tool fitted with a large scythe blade and fingers of wood to handle the grain. These deposited the straw in a row to the left of and behind the cradler. It was raked into bundles with a hand-rake, tied and set up in "stooks." It took a good man to swing a cradle from sunup to sundown.

The corn was cut by hand and set up in large bundles, presenting a haunting autumnal picture among the big, yellow pumpkins that usually grew in the corn fields. Later, this corn was drawn to the barn and set up against stout poles attached to stakes driven into the ground. This created a convenient tunnel in which the smaller children could crawl and play games whenever a few minutes could be spared for play.

Still later, the grain-bearing ears were picked from the corn-stalks and taken into the barn or cooper shop, where they were husked by hand with the help of a "husking pin" which penetrated the tough outside covering and made the extraction of the golden ears much easier. Husking bees, of which much has been written by historians and poets, were then in vogue, and were the source of much socializing and enjoyment by the entire neighborhood.

When the winter months set in with the attendent let-up of farm work, usually a few weeks could be spared for the young folks to attend school and at least acquire a smattering of education. Most rural dwellers never progressed much above the fourth or fifth grade level, a very few went on to high school, very many never learned to read or write. A very small percentage of the more affluent went on to college.

Let it not be thought, however, that life was all work and no play for the younger set of those old days. Social life, while limited, was greatly cherished and highly valued. Generally speaking, the church was the main social

116

medium that brought people together. Usually everyone who lived within a reasonable distance of a church, and that sometimes meant several miles, attended services on Sunday, and much visiting was done afterward. The churches were also instrumental in the forming of singing classes that gave periodic songfests, and elocution groups that organized "speakin's." These affairs were usually well attended, and many of the "singin's and speakin's" led to "sparkin's" that terminated in romance and marriage.

The schools also did their part by holding parties, spelling bees, and box socials. These also often led to the pairing off of certain couples, with the ultimate result of long and happy marriages.

For the outdoor-minded, and what youth wasn't in those days, there was plenty of hunting, fishing, and trapping. Henry's father personally disapproved of these activities as a waste of time; but not so Henry and his brother, and the other boys of the neighborhood. Often on rainy mornings in the summer they were allowed to go trout fishing, with the adjuration that if the weather cleared, they were supposed to return home and resume their normal duties. But, somehow, in spite of solemn promises, this seldom happened.

A rainy morning was a rainy day to them. Two good trout streams, the Fox and Deer Creeks, ran parallel with one another and about half a mile apart. The boys would fish down one for a couple of miles, cross over the intervening ridge, and fish back up the other. If they tired of fishing they would stop and go in swimming, or they played games; anything to delay their arrival home to around choretime. Their laxity in noticing changes in the weather was usualy forgiven, because they never failed to bring home a good mess of trout for the family.

With the exception of the fish-hooks, which cost two cents each, most of their tackle was homemade. Lines were made by an intricate process of twisting the long hairs from a horse's tail through a goose or turkey quill. Some of the more gifted line makers knew the art of making "salt-and-pepper" hued lines by combining both black and white horsehairs. These lines were very strong and durable, and being a little on the stiff side, had the admirable quality of sliding off branches and other obstructions instead of twisting around them.

Fish-poles were sometimes of carefully shaved ash or birch, but usually they were cut right where the fishing began. No flies or artificial lures were used, the good old-fashioned garden worm being considered the very best bait for trout. And with a fish on, nobody bothered to "play" it. It was evicted from its native element by a strong-arm sweep of the pole that sometimes sent it flying yards back into the meadows or bushes. Very often the smaller children were kept busy retrieving these high flying unfortunates. And now and then someone would train a pet dog to take over these duties. But if a fish was lost, it made very little difference, as there was always another one to take its place.

Henry Lyman related an incident that graphically illustrated the plentitude of trout in those days. He told how he and a group of companions were swimming and diving in a deep hole in Fox Creek, when suddenly one of the boys decided that he would rather fish. Without bothering to dress, he picked up his fishpole and pulled out eighty trout, running from six ounces to one pound in weight, as fast as he could bait his hook. This from the same hole in which the rest of the group were cavorting like otters, and in the course of less than an hour.

He also related how, in the early years of his parents' abode in the old homestead, his mother had a favorite fishing hole below a bridge near the sawmill, that she called her "pork barrel hole." Whenever she failed to have meat for a meal, or preferred fish, she could always

118

depend on getting all the fish she needed by a few minutes' fishing in this hole.

Small game was also plentiful, but powder and shot for the old muzzle-loading firearms of the day cost money. So, much game was taken by the use of snares and deadfalls. Passenger pigeons, once so numerous in northern New York, had already begun their decline toward eventual extinction, but there were still enough of them passing through during their annual mating and migratory flights to furnish an important source of food for those who chose to go after them. Henry used to listen in wonder to tales of the great flights of these birds, that were once so numerous that they would darken the light of the sun by their passing.

As time went by, Henry's father became more affluent, and he began to delegate much of his business on the farm and in the sawmills and store to his son-in-law and other trusted employees, while he devoted much of his own time to contracting the construction of buildings for others. One of these buildings, which he built in Lorraine Huddle, and which still stands, turned out to be financially unfortunate. Originally designed to be used as a church, the religious group for which it was built became insolvent before its completion, and Henry's father never received a penny for his work.

Nevertheless, he went ahead and finished the edifice, and then magnanimously presented it to the village. During the ensuing years it was used for a variety of purposes. For many years it was the Lorraine Town Hall, and at present it houses the Lorraine Fire Department.

Also during these later years, just preceding the Civil War, the elder Lyman became more and more involved in politics, both local and national. A rabid Abolitionist, he disagreed with many of the Presidents' ideas, and made his own beliefs known in many fiery speeches de-

119

livered at Abolitionist meetings. He was also engaged in certain secret activities about which Henry learned in a way that he never forgot.

One rainy day in summer he was engaged in constructing some juvenile contraption, when he happened to think of something that he needed which was stored in the attic of the old house. Access to this storage space was gained by a ladder and a trapdoor from an upstairs hallway. Climbing the ladder, Henry pushed up the trapdoor and stuck his head up through the opening. As soon as his eyes became adjusted to the change of lighting, he noted something moving between himself and a window at the other end of the attic, and to his horror, found himself staring into the face of a huge, black woman, who was sitting upon a box and calmly combing her hair.

Scared half out of his wits, Henry slammed down the hatch cover and scrambled downstairs, where he excitedly related to his mother what he had seen. She sat down and calmly explained to him that they knew the woman was there; that she was an escaped slave from a southern plantation whom they were hiding until an opportunity presented itself for them to forward her on her way to Canada and freedom.

That was the first inkling that Henry had that he was living in a station of the infamous Underground Railroad. And for many months afterward he never failed to cast a cautious eye upward whenever he passed beneath that trapdoor in the upstairs hallway.

This is the environment that Henry Lyman grew up in. Fortunate enough to receive more than the average amount of education, he went on to make an impressive mark in the world. In 1900 he privately published his memoirs in a very limited edition of fifty volumes. Today there are possibly five known copies still in exist-

120

ence, all highly valued by their owners. Fortunate indeed is anyone who is privileged to read one of these, and to live again the unique experience of growing up on Tug Hill.

HUCKLEBERRY CHARLIE, THE SAGE OF PINE PLAINS

"Come on folks . . git yer huckleberries. These huckleberries was picked on Pine Plains, couple miles this side of Great Bend. Guaranteed to be free of sticks and stones, stems and bruises. Step up, kind people, and purchase a few, for this is my last time through. Git yer huckleberries."

So sounded the sales chant from the little park on Public Square in Watertown, and quickly a crowd gathered around the tall, angular figure of the vendor. Hat rakishly cocked on one side, he stood with one hand holding a large cigar while the other busily dipped huckleberries from a milk-pail into quart containers. The folks knew that even though they purchased not an ounce of the succulent berries, they were in for some witty repartee. For this was "Huckleberry Charlie," noted philosopher, wit, and poet who hailed from Pine Plains, up near Great Bend.

"How's business, Charlie?" asked an acquaintance who stood nearby.

"Well, I'll tell you," returned Charlie. "I'm sellin' my berries and I'll go home with quite a lot of spondulix (money). Ain't gettin' all I expected, but then, I didn't expect to."

"I do business on a capital called wind, and manage to keep my head above warm water. Don't bore with a big augar, but I have just as many shavings as the most of 'em when night comes. The stars are high and the sky

123

is low. If the wind changes it'll rain 'fore morning for sure."

His name was Charles Sherman, and he was born February 15, 1842, the son of a prosperous Watertown family. His father, Eli Sherman, was a Wall Street commission merchant and brother to John A. Sherman who donated to the YMCA the site on which its building in Watertown now stands.

When Charlie was very young his parents both died, and he was brought up by his maternal grandparents, Mr. and Mrs. Thomas Reed of Great Bend. As he grew up he came to know and love every nook and cranny of that vast, level expanse of sand and trees known as Pine Plains, situated near his home and now a part of Camp Drum. On this tract grew thousands of huckleberry bushes, and young Charlie learned just where the largest and sweetest berries grew.

Eventually he learned that these berries had a monetary value, and countless pails of them were picked and delivered to surrounding villages, and to Watertown, where some of his best sales were made. Naturally, in time the name of "Huckleberry Charlie" attached itself to him, and it stuck for the rest of his life.

Charlie made hosts of friends wherever he went. People were attracted to his neat and upright, almost haughty, bearing; his natural instinct of independence and industry. But most of all they loved his sense of humor, his sparkling and ever-ready wit, and his ability to give vent to both by bursts of rapid-fire rhetoric that seemed to go on endlessly and always left his listeners laughing.

Charlie's repartee was usually innocuous and nonpersonal. But he could, if the occasion required, turn on a brand of vitriolic wit that could cause a heckler's toes to curl up, and leave him to sizzle in the tried-out fat of his own audacity. After this had been witnessed a few

124

times, people learned not to poke fun at Huckleberry Charlie.

He dearly loved to answer questions in comparative similies. Someone might say to him, "How are things, Charlie?" and like as not he might answer, "Slippin' fine, just like soapsuds down a sink." Or perhaps, "Slicker'n a mink mitten."

An acquaintance once said to him, "Nice night out, Charlie."

"Yup, rather nice overhead," agreed Charlie, "but there ain't very many travelin' that way." (Obviously, this was before the days of air travel.)

"The nights are sure getting longer," pursued the acquaintance.

"Yeah, they sure are," retorted Charlie. "Wisht I lived where they have six months night and six months day. Like to get there about sundown, so's I could get a good night's sleep. Hate to get there about sunup, though. Be a hell of a long time before dinner."

Charlie sold another commodity for which he was famous. This was his horseradish, and for it he had another catchy sales spiel.

"Git yer horseradish here. This is the finest horseradish that ever grew. Guaranteed to be the pure quill. Nothing taken away and nothing added except vinegar. Dug it and grated it myself. It's so strong that when I grated it the tears fell from my eyes like rain. And grated so fine that not once in the seventeen years that I've been selling it has anyone been able to find a piece of turnip in it the size of a pin head."

One of Charlie's weaknesses was for loud and gaudy clothing. A couple of times a year he would visit the clothing merchants of Watertown and make the announcement, "This is my birthday. Gotta git me some new clothes." Of course he had no intention of buying anything new, and the merchants knew this as well as anyone else. So they would dig out all the laid-away, un-salable articles of clothing that they could find and give them to him.

This custom led to some unbelievably comical sartorial combinations that greatly amused his friends. One time he went to the Watertown fair wearing a brilliant green suit, flaring red vest, yellow button shoes, and a derby hat much too large but padded with paper to hold it up off his ears.

The fair officials never charged him for admittance to the grounds. He was sort of a tradition there, and the concessionnaires all liked to have him stand in front of their stands, as a crowd always gathered around him. Needless to say, Charlie dearly loved all this attention.

He also loved to watch the harness racing, but said he didn't dare get too close to the track for fear his clothing might scare the horses.

When the United States Army took over Pine Plains as a training center for tactical maneuvers, it pained Charlie grievously to see columns of marching troops and horse-drawn artillery tearing up many of his beloved huckleberry bushes. But the excitement helped to make it bearable, and he soon became friends with most of the soldiers. Rank and high brass meant nothing to him; a man was merely a man. And most of them loved to hear him talk.

During the summer of 1908 the army at Pine Plains divided into groups of "Reds" and "Blues," and spent several days practicing tactical maneuvers against one another. One hot day the red army was concealed in a piece of woods waiting for the crucial moment to dash out and capture a large contingent of blues. Suddenly the blue commander saw Charlie approaching on a dead run.

"Wait," he shouted. "That there piece of woods is plumb full of fellers with red bands on their hats." Of

126

course the blue army's commander immediately gave orders to counteract and thwart the red army's plans.

This greatly infuriated the red commander, who swore at Charlie and called him all sorts of names, all in the German language. But this didn't ruffle a hair on Charlie, who didn't understand German anyway.

And even when someone told him that he was guilty of all sorts of crimes against the government, including treason punishable by death before a firing squad, he remained unperturbed.

"As long as them fellows with blue on their hats don't let me go hungry," he declared, "I ain't goin' to stand by and watch them all git captured."

The official report on the incident offered by the red commander was that his plans were upset by "information furnished to the blue troops by a friendly native."

Huckleberry Charlie Sherman died on January 15, 1921, and the Great Bend Baptist Church was crowded to overflowing on the day of his funeral, as hundreds of friends came to pay their last respects. And in this case, "respect" was not simply a figure of speech. Most of those who knew him did really respect him as a fine gentleman who brought them lots of enjoyment by his amusing antics and sayings. He is buried in Sunnyside Cemetery in Great Bend.

THE BURIED TREASURE
OF RODMAN

Probably only a very few of the oldest residents of
Rodman Township remember the old tale that used to
be told about a buried pot of English gold that for years
excited the imagination of the natives, but flouted all
their efforts to recover it. It even attracted treasure hunters from distant parts, but their efforts were no more
successful than those of the natives. Even to this day, no
one knows for sure that it was ever found.

The story really began with the defeat of St. Leger's
expedition against Fort Stanwix (Rome) during the
American Revolution. When the retreat to Canada began, the army apparently did not remain intact, but
broke up into several contingents, each taking a slightly
divergent route but all intent upon quickly reaching the
safety of Fort Frontenac, many miles to the north.

One of these segments had been attended by a band
of Iroquois warriors, whose home was an encampment
on the north branch of Big Sandy Creek, near where the
village of Rodman now stands. The route of this retreat-
ing band was through this encampment, and upon reaching it, the British officer in charge decided to pause for a
brief but much-needed rest. Here it was also decided to
abandon such cumbersome equipment as they could do
without; and this included a quantity of gold pieces in
charge of an army paymaster who happened to be with
them. Fear that the American forces whom they thought
to be hotly pursuing them would capture the money also
aided in making this decision. It was agreed that this

gold would be buried where it would be readily recoverable at some more propituous time in the future, when the American rebels had been put down and danger of capture by them had passed.

Accordingly, the paymaster, accompanied by one soldier, crept out of camp in the dead of night, taking with them the gold contained in a large, three-legged camp kettle. Near a spring that they decided would be readily remembered, they dug a hole and deposited the kettle with its golden burden. After covering it securely and camouflaging the spot, they crept back to camp; the only two men in all the world who knew of its whereabouts.

Apparently the vagaries of war prevented either of these men from returning to reclaim the treasure. The rebels were not put down, and the region never again returned to British domination. But about fifty years later, long after the war was ended, and even a second war with Great Britain had swept across the north country, a stranger suddenly appeared in the neighborhood, armed with maps, divining rods, and other equipment designed for locating buried treasure. This man made exhaustive inquiries concerning the exact location of the old Indian village, and thereafter did a lot of exploring and digging. Suddenly he disappeared — no one ever saw him again.

But by this time the magic secret was out. Buried treasure! What an inflammatory phrase in a small country village. Instantly everyone was treasure-conscious, and according to one source, the surrounding farm land, normally very rich and productive, was soon rendered almost unworkable because of the many holes that had been dug. But nothing was ever found, so far as is actually known.

At least one trio of treasure hunters believed that the gold had been claimed by the Devil and was guarded by the Prince of Darkness, as evidenced by the failure of all

130

efforts to locate it. Therefor, they figured that some form of exorcism was necessary, and devised a plan that they thought would work.

The digging began at the agreed-upon spot at midnight in the dark of the moon. While two dug, the other marched around and around the spot, a Bible in one hand and a pack of playing cards in the other, muttering some mysterious incantation about the Devil staying away and the gold appearing. At least half of the charm seemed to be working — the Devid did not put in an appearance. But neither did the gold.

Now some joker with a well-developed sense of humor had learned of the plan, and had made other plans of his own. Sometime prior to the appearance of the gold seekers, this fellow had secreted himself in a clump of bushes a short distance to windward of the scene of impending operations. With him he brought an old sheet, a lump of brimstone, and a dish of live coals, covered with ashes to preserve their heat.

When the diggers had become well engrossed in their work, the hidden watcher blew the ashes from the coals and dropped the brimstone thereon. The breeze did the rest. Soon the sulphurous odor of hell-fire was wafting toward the busy workers, and one by one their nostrils picked it up. This, of course, caused them to be rather restless and apprehensive.

At about that time a white-clad figure detached itself from the clump of bushes, prancing wildly about and uttering unearthly cries. This, coupled with the smell of brimstone, was just a little too much. With one accord the three treasure hunters left their digging and their tools, and set out at top speed for the village and the companionship of other human beings. It is said that they told some wonderful tales about how close they came to being sucked down into the maw of Hell on that eventful night.

But the search went on for some time after that, until one day someone discovered a hole in the ground near a spring, and in the bottom of the hole there plainly showed the print of a three-legged kettle. It might have been pure coincidence that just about that time a local man, who had always been poor as a church mouse, suddenly moved to another locality and bought a large and prosperous farm.

If this individual did in fact find the treasure and put it to such a worthwhile purpose, well and good. But no further evidence in proof of this was ever discovered. In fact, the only coin ever found around Rodman that could be even remotely connected with the British army was one lonely English penny bearing the date 1771. However, after this the treasure fever quickly died out, and today the incident is hardly remembered.

BUCKETY STOUT AND
THE INVISIBLE OWL

He wasn't always known as Buckety Stout. In the neighborhood where he was born and brought up, near Fulton, New York, he was officially Floyd McDougal.

Later he migrated to upper Boylston, on the flank of Tug Hill, and here he met and married Mabel Beach, a granddaughter of one of the first settlers in the area. Having taken a great liking to the countryside, he bought the farm originally cleared and settled by his wifes' ancestors; near the Beach Schoolhouse on the Smartville road, and about a mile from the Catholic Church corners.

Here he lived for the remainder of his life, siring a large family of six healthy sons and nine daughters, who all received adequate educations, and were brought up in the tradition of self-reliance and personal ambition so prevalent in those times.

Here, also, he evolved many of the schemes necessary to provide him with the money to successfully raise such a large family. Being of Scotch ancestry, his independent nature prompted him to rebel against seeking or accepting any outside financial aid in this respect. This in itself seems almost incredible in this day and age, when one considers how very easy it is for present-day fathers far less deserving than he to obtain almost unlimited welfare aid in supporting their families.

Mr. McDougal scorned this. Instead, he put on his thinking cap and began to devise ways and means. The little farm, while furnishing part of the necessary provender, fell far short of being adequate to provide a decent living for so many, so other sources of income had to be developed. He used to say that he did his best planning late at night, when other folks were in bed enjoying their rest.

Whenever and however this planning was done, he certainly came up with a variety of money-making ideas. About the first of these to attract public attention was the invention of a killer- type animal trap which he patented and began to manufacture in a small basement shop in Lacona. This trap, while very effective in its purpose, did not pan out too well because of its weight and bulkiness, and after a short period was discontinued.

Then there was the invention of an ingenious door latch that was activated by the closing pressure of a hand. This effort was also aborted by lack of adequate capital for development and promotion.

Next he started a small establishment near his home for the manufacture of bushel wooden crates. Hundreds of these containers were built and sold, and were so sturdily constructed that many of them are still in existence.

Another project conjured up by his active brain was the preparation of rough and irregular pulpwood for sale to paper mills. This process involved the use of a rossing machine that removed the bark and projecting knots, and through it many spruce and hemlock trees that had hitherto been considered unsalable found their way into paper manufacturing plants.

Farmers were glad to dispose of their scrubby pasture and woodlot trees at almost any price, and this venture proved to be very profitable. Soon Mr. McDougal had his own trucks doing full-time hauling of this product to various outlets. But as has happened many times before, depletion of a ready supply of raw material finally wrote "finis' 'to the venture.

During these years, Mr. McDougal had also gone

into town politics, and was elected to the office of road commissioner (highway superintendent). He served in this capacity for a number of years, and many of the "improved roads" in the Town of Boylston were built by him. Some of these roads are still standing the test of time; thus attesting to the thoroughness of their builder's methods.

Probably Mr. McDougal's most spectacular venture, and certainly the one with the greatest profit potential, was the creation of McDougal's Deer Park. This came about during the later years of his life, and was his pride and joy. Unfortunately, it had just begun to yield profits at the time of his death.

Having acquired some two hundred acres of woods and brushland, through which there ran a sizable spring-fed creek, he proceeded to enclose this tract at considerable expense with a page-wire fence ten feet high. It was said that it took two box-car loads of wire to do the trick, and the labor alone must have involved a pretty penny. A back section of the fence was left unfinished to allow the escape of any wild deer that might be hiding inside. Then a couple of game wardens came, and with the help of a crew of volunteers, a thorough drive was made toward the opening. Once certain that no wild game remained inside, the gap was securely closed.

Then Mr. McDougal proceeded to stock the enclosure with his own breeding stock, purchased from commercial suppliers. He brought in several strains, even introducing a few European red deer, a species slightly smaller than the Adirondack white-tail but supposed to be very sturdy and durable. After a couple of years, when the stock had multiplied a bit, he obtained a license to sell venison, either by the pound or carcass, to individuals and eating places that desired to place this delicacy on their menus.

As I have said, this venture ended for Mr. McDougal

at his untimely death at the age of 53 years. However, the deer park lived on for some years after that. A company was formed by several stockholders and sons of the founder to continue the establishment, and quite an amount of venison was produced. However, most of the new owners had other jobs that prevented them from maintaining a regular patrol, or even a close watch, of the property. Probably poachers helped to deplete the stock to some extent; but deep snows and trees falling across the fence, aided the escape of many deer, and these facts, coupled with the increasing expense of maintaining the enclosure, brought the venture to an end quite some years ago.

For many years it was not an unusual sight to see from twenty to fifty deer of all ages and sizes, at a feeding station just across the road from Mr. McDougal's old home. A fitting memorial to an ambition and a dream!

Mr. McDouglas was short and very stoutly built; not fat, but composed of a good deal of muscle and sinew. His neck was short and thick, making him appear to have veritably no neck at all, and it was this peculiarity that prompted the nickname by which he was known for many years.

An Irish wit by the name of Pat Bailey, who lived two houses away, once said of him, "He's built like a bucket, and anyone can see that he sure is stout. He should have been named 'Buckety Stout'."

Well, the name caught on, as such things sometimes will, and it stayed with him, locally, for the rest of his days. Mr. McDougal realized that its use reflected no lack of respect for him and, as was his wont, he accepted it good-naturedly, along with its variations of Buck Stout and Buck McDougal.

Aside from his other attributes, Mr. McDougal was also known for his ready wit, and his liking for practical jokes. No matter what was said to him, he always had a ready and adequate answer, as many a would-be jokester found out to his own embarrassment. And the tricks that he sometimes played caused much merriment and are still recounted by the older residents of the area.

One of the best remembered of these was the incident of the invisible owl. It occurred while he was filling the office of road commissioner, and had a gang of men working on the road through the Beach Woods, within half a mile of his own home.

For some reason, he was poking about in the edge of the woods bordering the road, when he came upon the carcass of a freshly-killed great horned owl. Upon examination he found a bullet hole in the bird's body, and surmised that it had been shot some distance away and had flown to this point before succumbing to the wound.

As he stood looking at the bird, plans for a prank began forming in his agile mind. Cautiously looking back, he noted that his gang of road workers were some distance away and were apparently paying no attention to him or his actions. Assuming a nonchalant air, he sauntered back to where they were at work, passing a couple of casual remarks as he did so. Then all at once he spoke up excitedly.

"Will you look at the size of that owl," he exclaimed, pointing into the top of the tree right above where the dead bird lay. Everyone craned his neck, but, of course, try as they might, no one could see any owl.

"What ails you, Buck, have you gone crazy?" one man said. "There ain't no owl there."

"You mean to stand there and tell me you can't see that owl, right there in that tree?" asked Buck incredulously. "Something must ail your eyes. You can see him, can't you boys?" he asked, turning to the other men.

"Well, I sure can't," said one fellow. "Something must be wrong with *your* eyes, Buck. Can any of you fellers see an owl " he appealed to the others. All vowed that they could not.

"Now that sure does beat all," said Buck wonderingly, a serious expression on his face. "Here I've had a gang of blind men working for me, and never knew it before. Well, guess I'll have to prove it to you."

One of his younger sons, Floyd, Jr., had been hanging around with the workmen, and Buck now addressed him. "Floyd," he said, "run to the house and bring me my rifle and a couple shells. Hustle before he gets scairt and flies away."

Floyd was off like a shot, and Buck continued to watch the treetop intently. Every now and then one of the workers would offer the jocular query, "Is he still there, Buck?" and McDougal would reply in the affirmative.

Within ten minutes, Floyd was back with the rifle and cartridges. Buck never shifted his eyes from the treetop as he slipped a shell into the weapon. Then, dropping to one knee, he drew a careful bead on the invisible owl.

"Gotta aim real careful," he muttered. "Them cusses are more'n half feathers."

At the crack of the rifle he sprang up jubilantly. "I got him," he yelled. "Did you see him fall?"

Of course no one had, and many were the jeering remarks as they trooped after him toward the base of the tree. But jeers changed to exclamations of surprise and wonderment as their eyes fell upon the dead owl sprawled on the ground.

"Now boys, whose sight is off, yours or mine?" asked Buck of the wondering workmen, who were shaking their heads in bewilderment. Maybe, they figured, their sight was only normal, while Buck's was far above.

Finally, one of the men reached down and picked up the dead bird, and a crafty gleam came into his eyes.

138

"Why Buck," he said, "this bird musta been dead for a long time. He's stiff already."

"Sure he is," agreed Buck, his nimble wit once again coming to his rescue and pulling him out of a tight spot. "Hit 'em in the right spot and you'll knock 'em stiff every time."

THE PASSENGER PIGEONS

Nature has always been a bountiful provider for those of her children, both man and beast, who know how to take advantage of her generosity. Left to itself, the animal kingdom would strike its own balance and maintain its own parity. It is man who always through greed and ignorance, causes the imbalance that eventually upsets Nature's apple-cart.

Belatedly, man is coming to realize this glaring fact, and is slowly commencing to do something about it. But this self reform came too late to save the vast herds of buffalo that used to roam the western plains; almost too late to save the last remnants of this splendid species that a little over a hundred years ago was considered to be inexhaustible. And it took place much too late to save even a last remaining individual of another species that was once considered even more numerous than the buffalo—the passenger pigeon.

These magnificent birds, whose great flights used to actually darken the light from the sun, have for many decades supposedly been gone entirely from the face of the earth. The last known specimen died in the Cincinnati Zoological Gardens in 1914.

Passenger pigeons derived their name from the swiftness of their flight. According to one observer, "It seems that they are never here, but either coming or going," and the rapidity of their passage made them "passengers." Specimens killed near New York City were found to have their crops filled with rice which must have been eaten in the plantations of the Carolinas or Georgia. As this is a distance of from six to seven hundred

141

miles, and the grain would have digested in twelve hours, the birds must have traveled at a speed of about sixty miles an hour. This is a remarkable speed for long sustained flight.

The earliest known historical mention of pigeons was made in 1605 by Samuel DeChamplain, who noted that on the coast of Maine he encountered "an infinite number of pigeons," many of which were killed as food for his party. The Jesuit fathers recorded in 1610 that in Acadia the birds were as numerous as the fishes, and that "pigeons overloaded the trees." John Lawson in his "History of Carolina," 1709, speaks of "prodigious flocks of pigeons that broke down trees and cleared away all the food in the country before them."

In 1643 The Plymouth Colony was threatened by famine when great flocks of pigeons descended upon the fields of ripened corn and grain, and "broke down and devoured a great quantity." But in 1648 they came again, after the harvest this time, and proved a great blessing because of the much-needed meat which they provided.

In olden times hunting parties of Indians, including squaws and children, congregated in large numbers near pigeon nesting grounds. The birds were slaughtered in great quantities, and had been since time immemorial. Only the large, meaty breasts of the birds were saved, and the only way of preserving these was by smoking and drying. The fat from the squabs was fried out and preserved in earthen pots for use as butter as used by white men. Sometimes small villages possessed several hundred gallons of this delicacy.

The size of the adult passenger pigeon was about seventeen to eighteen inches in length. In coloring, the male bird was mostly bluish to brownish grey above, the breast and under sides being a reddish fawn, and the legs and feet a reddish purple. The female was of a somewhat duller coloration, being more brownish than bluish grey of the upper plumage, while below she was drab grey with less pronounced purplish hue to legs and feet. The general outline of the bird was trim and racy, greatly resembling the outline of present-day carrier pigeons, only on a larger scale.

These extremely gregarious birds nested in huge numbers in dense forests, sometimes building fifty to one hundred nests of twigs in a single tree. Often trees were stripped of their branches because of the weight of nesting birds, and the ground would be strewn with eggs and the bodies of young birds, which became food for wild hogs, bears, skunks, hawks, and other predators. Also, the ground might be inches deep in the guano from the birds, and a nesting place could be detected by the smell for long distances.

One authority indicates that each nesting produced only two pure white eggs, but nestings might occur several times each year. The two eggs hatched into a male and a female fledgling in eleven days. These birdlings, if both survived, were supposed to mate at maturity. If this was true, and the same rules that apply to mammals also apply to birds, it would seem that such inbreeding would eventually weaken the strain, and may have had something to do with the eventual extinction of the species. The young birds were able to reproduce their kind within about six months after hatching. The flocks were said to normally double, and sometimes triple, their size each year.

The male birds left the nesting places at daylight and flew off to the feeding grounds, returning about ten in the forenoon. Immediately they took their places on the nests, covering the eggs while the females went to feed. The females returned about three to four o'clock in the afternoon, and the males again went to feed, getting back anywhere from sundown until midnight. It is said that returning after dark, these husbands each flew unerringly to his own nest and mate, in spite of the confusion of hundreds of thousands of nests and the deafening hub-bub of millions of birds.

After the young were hatched and nearly full grown, both parent birds left the nesting areas to feed at sunrise. Both secreted in their crops a kind of milk or curd known as "pigeon milk," with which they fed the young until they were ready to fly. At this time they packed the young birds' crops with nuts, seeds, and grain until the size of the crop almost equalled that of the bird. After two days the young had become veritable masses of fat and were called squabs, and at this time they were pushed from the nests and left to fend for themselves. The parents then flew to new nesting grounds, sometimes a hundred or more miles away.

Providentially, the parent birds never foraged within many miles of the nesting places, leaving the food for the use of the young after they had been ejected from the nests and before they were able to fly long distances to feeding grounds. All kinds of nuts and acorns, wild berries and cherries, and the seeds of various trees and weeds, were consumed, as well as bugs, worms and snails. It is said that sometimes inch-worms and caterpillars were practically non-existent for several miles and several years around a spot where a nesting place had been. Orphaned young whose parents had been killed were usually cared for by the adults of neighboring nests.

Nesting migrations might take place several times a year, but the great general migrations from one geographical division to another, like from north to south or vice-versa, took place twice annually, in March and in late fall. During these migrations, flocks built up to incredible size. Alexander Wilson, father of American ornithology, told of observing one flight which he estimated to be over a mile wide and about two hundred and forty miles long. Allowing two birds to each cubic yard

144

of flying space, he calculated this flock to contain about two billion, two hundred and thirty million, two hundred and seventy-two thousand birds. On the supposition that each bird consumed half a pint of food per day, such a flock, he calculated, would require seventeen million, four hundred and twenty-four thousand bushels of food each day.

Fortunate indeed that this gentleman could deal in such astronomical figures. Fortunate also that the diet of these birds consisted chiefly of wild materials. However, in the later years of their existence, after huge grain fields had developed in the midwest, many farmers were forced to guard their crops during migratory seasons.

Audubon related that in the autumn of 1813 he observed a huge flight of pigeons near the Ohio River that obscured the light of the mid-day sun like an eclipse. His estimation was that this flock, allowing two birds to each cubic yard of space, one mile wide and traveling at sixty miles per hour, contained one billion, two hundred and fifteen million, one hundred and thirty-six thousand indivdiuals; and that they would require eight million, seven hundred and twelve thousand bushels of food each day.

Mr. Audubon stated that these flights continued for three days, and he also mentioned visiting a "resting place" near Green River, Kentucky. Quoting Mr. Audubon: "The noise that they made in flight reminded me of the passage of sea-breeezes through the cordage of a ship at sea, and the current of air created by their wings as they passed overhead greatly astonished me . . . "Fires were lighted to guide them in, and they continued to arrive without intermission. The birds precipitated themselves wherever they could, one upon another, in masses the size of barrels, until the branches of the trees gave way under their weight . . . "Thousands were struck down by men and boys with poles, and the tumult and

145

confusion was so great that I could not converse with men nearest me. I could not hear the sound of the guns, and only perceived that the men had fired by seeing them reloading their weapons."

Whenever a nesting or feeding place was established, people for miles around gravitated to the area to share in the harvest. Sometimes several hunters would band together, forming a sort of working group, and these groups might follow a flock from one nesting ground to another. They were known as professional "pigeoners," and especially after railroads had penetrated to some of the more isolated sections, they shipped millions of these birds to restaurants and other outlets in big cities. Here they found ready markets, as they were considered a delicacy.

Often whole families, or several combined families, would move to the vicinity of a nesting ground, bringing with them teams and wagons loaded with camping gear, provisions, barrels, and salt. Here they would stay for several days or weeks, the men killing the birds by any means possible, and the women and children dressing them and packing the flesh in salt in the barrels. In these cases the meaty breasts were usually the only parts used, thus devoting more space to food and less to bones. When enough meat had been accumulated, the groups would pull out for home, taking with them a goodly part of the years' meat supply.

During the mating season, pigeons were very fond of salty mud and water. Knowing of this, professional pigeoners took advantage of this fact by salting mud flats, over which they spread their nets. These nets were by far the fastest and most efficient method of taking large numbers of birds, also the cheapest. After all, powder and shot cost money and could soon eat up a large portion of the profits; and the mere act of loading and firing guns at such sure targets soon palled upon the

146

enthusiasm of even the most dedicated hunters.

Made from light but strong cords, the nets were set over either the salted mud flats or baited spots near feeding grounds. They were supported on each corner by four long, light poles, the bottoms of which were interconnected by strong cords in such a manner that a good yank on a single rope would topple the whole structure onto the ground below.

Then the operator, trip-rope in hand, secreted himself in a nearby hiding place and waited. When a flock arrived the birds were quick to cluster beneath the nets in a mad scramble for the grain or salty water. When the operator decided that the time was ripe, he would yank the rope, after which he could wring the necks of the entrapped pigeons at leisure.

Sometimes one of these nets would capture hundreds of birds at a time, and when one considers that there might be dozens of them in operation near a feeding area, one begins to get an idea of the magnitude of the slaughter perpetrated in this manner.

Of course there were other methods of taking the birds. At the height of the pigeon population many of them could be killed by a single discharge of a shotgun. One case on record cites seventy-two taken with two shots, and a single shot from a flintlock, fired into a tree, brought down a backload of birds.

One story concerns a man who lived near Constableville, whose house stood on a high hill. One day he noticed the vanguard of a huge flight of pigeons approaching, and perceiving that they would pass his place at a very low altitude, he decided to try to secure some of the succulent birds for his family's use. Having no gun, he had to resort to other measures.

Accordingly, he wired a broom fast to a long pole, and climbed upon his roof with the improvised weapon. Here he tied himself fast to the chimney, and in the next

147

hour, while the flight was passing over, succeeded in knocking down over seventy birds. Meanwhile, his wife and children were busy on the ground, chasing and dispatching the injured and gathering them up in baskets. It was said that this family lived very highly for a few days at least.

It seems incredible that these forays, especially on the nesting places, should not scare the birds into leaving for other parts, but apparently this did not happen. The species was never noted for its great display of intelligence, and in the terrific noise and hub-bub of a nesting area, often extending for miles, the sound of firearms and the activities of the hunters was said to have gone virtually unnoticed.

A great slaughter of pigeons is said to have taken place in New York State in the late 1870's. This flight had nested on the upper reaches of the Beaverkill, in Ulster County, and because of the advent of the railroads, were within easy shipping distance of New York City. Millions of them were killed and dressed, packed in ice, and rushed to markets there. One source states that over one hundred and fifty tons of ice were used in the transportation of the squabs alone.

In spite of this continual persecution by man, it still seems incredible that such immeasurable numbers of these highly gregarious creatures could have been reduced to actual extinction in a few short years. Much discussion and speculation, and many theories dealing with the mystery have been put forth by ornithologists, naturalists, and bird lovers in general.

Many maintain that immense flocks were blown out to sea by gales and drowned by the millions, as attested to by great numbers of floating bodies having been seen far out in the Atlantic by seafarers. This is also supposed to have happened in the Great Lakes, especially Lakes Michigan and Superior, where vast windrows of drowned

The Catholic Church at Highmarket, built in the days when churches flung their steeples proudly to the skies. *(Photo by the author)*

An abandoned Tug Hill farm house. *(Photo by the author)*

The Old Homestead, boyhood home of H. H. Lyman. Wing on back of house has been removed. *(Photo by the author)*

This building stands on site of Old Corner Store where F. W. Woolworth first began work as clerk, and where first five-cent counter was introduced. Built by Mr. Woolworth early in century, the ground floor was used for five-and-ten until recently. *(Photo by the author)*

The Woolworth Memorial Church at Great Bend, N. Y. *(Photo by the author)*

The Sandy Creek Valley cheese factory, where famous Rodman (Heath) cheese is still made. This is one of only two family-run cheese plants left in New York State. In 1898 there were about 1,300. *(Photo courtesy Eric J. Dutton)*

Orrin N. Heath, dean of New York State cheese makers. Still dedicated at 91. *(Photo courtesy Eric J. Dutton)*

The Croghan Meat Market, home of Croghan bologna, in 1927. *(Photo courtesy of Campany Brothers)*

Croghan bolognas curing in wood smoke. *(Photo courtesy Campany Brothers)*

Nelson (Nett) Clifford, Greenborough's top
bear hunter. *(Photo courtesy Mrs. Corrine
Hasseler)*

Bert Clifford and a friend. *(Photo
courtesy Mrs. Corrine Hasseler)*

Nelson and Julia Clifford, last owners of the
famous old Cottrell Hotel at Greenborough.
(Photo courtesy Mrs. Corrine Hasseler)

Claude Clifford with a friendly bear cub.
(Photo courtesy Mrs. Corrine Hasseler)

Huckleberry Charlie, the Sage of Pine Plains.
(Watertown Daily Times photo)

The original Moore store in Lorraine as it looked in 1893. Store and hotel at right burned in 1894 but Mr. Moore rebuilt on another location. Present Moore store, run by C. C. Moore's grandson, Donald, is situated just out of picture at right. In picture from left to right are Dr. W. C. Fawdrey, Mrs. C. C. Moore and son, Frank, with C. C. Moore sitting in chair holding grandson Perry. At left of door is F. E. Macomber, a store employee, and standing in door is Jacob Chrysler of Rodman. Carrie Moore is in upstairs window. Seated on peddler's cart is Edward Moore, another son of C. C. Moore. Note brooms carried on top of cart, also crates carried for eggs taken in trade. *(Photo courtesy of Richard Knobloch)*

The old inn and stage stop at Denmark, still a beautiful landmark. *(Photo by author)*

Swancott's Mills — on the West Leyden-Osceola road.

birds were found washed up on certain remote shore-lines.

Others argue that continued disturbance of the nesting places by man finally forced the flocks to take refuge in the then comparatively undisturbed wilderness of northern Canada. There, they say, cold and unsatisfactory nesting conditions and unseasonable storms practically exterminated them.

While any or all of these may be true, it is much more plausible to accept the theories of the group who contend that the indiscriminate killing of the young, year after year, coupled with the destruction of the great pine, beech and oak forests that furnished a large part of the pigeons' diet, finally brought about the ultimate end of the species.

It is known that from the 1850's on a sharp diminution of the large flights was noted along the eastern seaboard. In the midwestern states this reduction was not seriously apparent for a few more years, but by the beginning of the twentieth century even here the flocks had become far between and small, numbering hundreds of birds instead of billions. Inside of another decade they had disappeared altogether, except for the one lone captive which died in the Cincinnati Zoo.

While officially the breed is dead, there are those of us who like to believe that this may not be so. According to "Birds of America," these birds sometimes migrated "accidentally" to regions far removed from their usual habitat. It is not inconceivable that storms or hurricanes might have blown flights caught over open water off course, and it is known that they were sometimes seen as far afield as Europe, the British Isles, Bermuda, and Cuba.

Why then is it not possible that some of these straying flights might have wandered into the jungles and rain forests of South America? It would seem that if this should have happened, the birds would have found conditions ideal for their way of life, and they would have stayed there. And certainly, with the limited access of white men to these regions, they might still exist in large numbers totally undetected by any but native Indians, to whom they would be just another part of everyday life.

Perhaps sometime a plane flying low over some Amazonian jungle may encounter a great flight of birds that will turn out to be, once again, Passenger Pigeons.

SALT PORK AND
JOHNNY-CAKE

In the lives of pioneer families, much more than in those of today, diet played an all-important part. To withstand the rigors of primitive living, bodies had to be fortified with far more sturdy edibles than are thought necessary or desirable in present times.

These foodstuffs must necessarily possess three qualities in common: they must be readily accessible, or producable; they must be rich in energy-giving potentials; and they must be easily preserved and transported. Flavor was an asset desirable but relatively unimportant. In those days, eating was more a matter of survival than of enjoyment. And anyway, the hard grinding labor of clearing and working a backwoods farm, or work in the lumbering woods, or following a trap-line in all kinds of weather, generated ravenous appetites that largely negated any concessions to delicacy of taste.

In the very beginning of the invasion of white men into the Tug Hill area, the qualities of durability and portability outweighed all the others. Sojourners into the wilderness must carry several days rations with them, usually in a knapsack slung over a shoulder. Thus it was that many a hunter, trapper, or scout set out on a protracted journey carrying only a few pounds of jerked venison, a pint of parched corn, and a small packet of salt as his only provisions. These items were light and nourishing, and with the exception of the salt, practically indestructible.

However, by the time that settlement had reached a

stage where whole families were moving in and establishing themselves, these primitive standbys had given way to slightly more advanced methods. True, the basic diet ingredients remained about the same. Venison and bear meat were staples; fresh, smoked, and dried. So was corn, but instead of being parched, it was now taken to the various grist-mills that sprang up, where it was ground into coarse meal or hominy. And, as nearly every settler now raised hogs, pork was taking a prominent place in everyday fare.

It was about this time that salt pork and johnny-cake came into their own as year-in, year-out standbys. Both were filling and nourishing and easily prepared, and both were readily come by.

Salt pork, also known as salty, sowbelly, salt horse, and white tiger, was derived from all those parts of a hog left over after the hams and shoulders were pickled or smoked. These were placed in a brine salty enough to float an unbroken egg, and left there for five or six weeks. At the end of this period, the finished product had absorbed enough salt to insure its keeping no matter how hot or unfavorable the weather became. And this was an essential quality, as no refrigeration, other than that furnished by a cool spring or well, was known at that time. A very few of the more opulent citizens might possess ice-houses in which blocks of ice might be preserved in saw-dust for part of the summer; but these were few and far between.

However, the extreme saline quality of pork so preserved posed a problem of its own, as few could abide its unmitigated saltiness. Therefor, it was necessary to "freshen' 'it by placing the sliced product in a frying pan, adding enough water to cover it, and bringing the water to a boil. This removed most of the salt, after which the slices were fried to a crisp, golden brown. When served with boiled potatoes, milk gravy, and johnny-cake, they

152

provided a delicious and nourishing meal. The salt pork grease thus obtained was much valued as a gravy on potatoes, corn bread, or vegetables.

Sometimes salt pork was cut into small square chunks, and cooked with cabbage, string beans, and dandelion or cowslip greens; thus imparting a rich flavor to the vegetables.

Although some of the more well-to-do families often enjoyed beef or mutton, salt pork came to be by far the most heavily consumed meat product in the rural areas, especially in the lumber camps. Cattle were considered far too valuable to be slaughtered for food, except on such rare occasions as when one broke a leg or met with some other accident. And a sheep converted into mutton, of course, ceased to yield the valuable wool from which most of a rural family's winter clothing was made. But hogs were plentiful and easily raised, and having once been butchered, easily preserved. So it of course followed that salt pork should assume the popularity that it gained as a rural standby.

Salt pork's inveterate companion, johnny-cake, seems to have originated in the New England States and invaded the Tug Hill area along with the settlers that came from that region. Originally called "journey cake," it was a readily-concocted, long lasting, and easily transported type of corn bread that became very popular with travelers who had to carry their sustenance with them, either afoot or on horseback. As is usually the case, the name was altered from time to time, and finally became "johnny-cake."

The first journey cakes were simply and easily concocted from an unleavened mixture of corn meal and water with a pinch of salt thrown in, and baked almost anywhere from a brick oven to a covered skillet on the hearthstone of a fireplace. Many have been baked on a flat stone beside a glowing campfire. Corn being one of

153

the most nutritious of grains, a traveler could subsist for days on this food alone, if necessary, and it could be carried for long periods of time without spoiling.

As the settlement of the wilderness became more extensive, the basic qualities of johnny-cake insured its popularity with settlers who came to stay. However, it was thereafter experimented with and refined by the addition of some type of leavening, perhaps an egg for lightness, and a little sugar or honey to improve the taste. And it is still a prime favorite among hundreds of folks all over the country who were born and raised in the rural and backwoods regions of America.

A one-time variation of johnny-cake was said to have originated with the Iroquois Indians, and was known as "Ingun Bread." This product was somewhat more soggy and heavy-grained than regular johnny-cake, and had a distinctly different taste, savoring more of the original corn flavor. A peculiar quality of this food was the fact that the more one chewed it, the better it tasted; and the writer can attest to the truth of this. Usually it was baked in a round-bottomed iron kettle, and it was said that a half-inch-thick slice cut from one of these loaves would sustain a large man throughout a full day of hard manual labor.

Many persons living today, among them millionaires and paupers, musicians and bankers, writers and merchant princes, had their beginnings in humble surroundings wherein salt pork and johnnycake were everyday fare. Yet, today, if one should drop into almost any restaurant in the land and ask for either of these old-time standbys, he would be greeted by either blank stares of incomprehension, or the pitying looks usually reserved for those of inferior mentality.

But the fact remains that in many backwoods kitchens, either or both may be come across occasionally, if

154

one is lucky. And the added fact that salt pork and johnnycake played an important part in the life and development of Tug Hill country, as well as many other communities across the land, cannot be denied.

WEATHERWISE . . .
AND OTHERWISE

In these days of modern scientific miracles, our national weather bureau boasts that they can tell us just what the weather is going to be in any specific place, either fifteen minutes or several days in advance. By the use of ultra-advanced equipment such as weather spotting planes, wind gauges, barometric pressure indicators, and so forth, they claim to be able to tell if the weather will be suitable for a space-flight blastoff next month or for your family picnic this coming Sunday.

Usually they are right, but there have been instances where they have failed dismally. A notable example of this occurred a few years ago during a World Series game. Hardly had the contest gotten under way when a heavy downpour sent the players scurrying for cover. But the weather bureau said it was nothing to worry about; that in twenty minutes the sun would come out and the game could be resumed.

However, this did not prove to be the case. The rain continued for two more solid days, and it was not until the third day that the championship play could go on. This goes to prove that nothing, no matter how scientific, is infallible.

But so much have people come to depend upon the weather reports that are broadcast every few minutes on radio and television, that the ability to forecast weather by the old-fashioned method of observing natural signs and conditions has almost ceased to exist. True, a few old-timers are still adept in this method, and can yet rival

157

the scientific gadgets in accuracy. But these individuals are becoming few and far between.

Time was, and not so very many years ago, when any person to whom the forthcoming weather was of prime importance, had to rely upon his own intuition and judgment based on his observation and knowledge of "weather signs." This ability was of special value to farmers, of which the larger percentage of the population consisted at that time. For instance, it was poor judgment to cut down several acres of hay if the weather signs pointed to a few days of wet weather. And it was wasteful to spray the potatoes with bug poison if an impending shower threatened to wash it all off again. So farmers especially made a study of weather signs and portents, and trained their young sons in the art almost from boyhood.

Of course it was a fact that different sets of signs were used in different localities, or that slightly different meanings were attached to the same ones. But by and large, the general interpretations of the principal indications were essentially the same, and were recognized the country over.

As an example, the saying "Curdly sky, not long dry" meant the same in Texas, Michigan, or on Tug Hill; specifically, that when the sky was filled with small, close-together, broken clouds, it meant that rain was imminent, usually within twenty-four hours. This, of course, was a "summer-time sign" in the northern climes, as such conditions rarely occurred in winter.

Likewise, in summer, when the leaves of the trees showed their undersides, this also meant rain within a few hours. If the setting sun dropped into a bank of clouds, very likely it would rain tomorrow. And certainly, without fail, it would rain again tomorrow if the sun shone while a brief shower was going on today.

The old saying "Rainbow at night, sailor's delight,"

was not confined entirely to the seafarer's idiom. Farmers also knew that a rainbow in the evening presaged a fine day on the morrow, and they could safely plan a big day's work. And transversely, they also knew that a rainbow during the early morning hours meant a wet and stormy day ahead. What would have happened if these two portents had occurred consecutively is not a matter of history.

If one arose early in the morning and found the rain pelting down, he could quite safely plan an outdoor job for the afternoon. For "Rain 'fore seven, stop 'fore 'leven" was a recognized rule, and to be perfectly truthful, it usually worked out that way.

The absence of any sign of dew upon the grass in early morning warned that there would be plenty of other moisture in the form of rain before another dawn rolled around. And if the sun came out particularly hot and scalding after a brief shower, no one at all weather-wise ever believed that it would remain fair for very long. For that was a sure sign that more rain would follow within a half hour or so.

The light-colored, usually oblique, streaks in the sky caused by the hidden sun shining through rents in the clouds, were said by old-time weather prophets to be "the sun drawing water," and were sure signs of rain within a day or so. Strange to say, although the cause is known to have been fallacious, the result was usually as predicted.

And in the days when wood was the almost universal type of fuel used in farm homes, sparks snapping and resnapping from a stove or fireplace almost infallibly predicted rain, especially in winter.

There were many other indications of coming precipitation that were exclusive to the winter months. If the smoke from chimneys rose straight up, dry and cold weather was coming. But if it settled down and lay in a thick blanket a few feet above the ground, watch for a thaw, and probably rain.

Also, if the trees in the forest took on a very dark appearance, when viewed from a distance, or were covered with a white hoar-frost in early morning, then the same conditions, thaw with rain, could be expected within the next thirty-six hours.

When water drawn from a well in winter had a warm and insipid flavor, it meant that a spell of extremely cold weather was in store. But on the other hand, if the water was unusually cold and bracing it indicated just the opposite . . . warm weather, and probably rain.

When "sun dogs," small colored spots in the sky to the left and right of the sun, were seen in winter, folks prepared themselves for a storm of some kind, usually a blizzard. The distance that the "dogs" appeared from the sun was said to indicate the approximate lapse of time before the start of the storm. If these spots appeared in summer, it meant that a rainy spell was in store.

Likewise, a light-colored, hazy circle around the moon presaged a storm of some kind; and also in this case the length of time before the storm's start was indicated by the distance that the circle appeared from the moon. Some of the more superstitious viewers reckoned this time by the number of stars that appeared within the circle, each star representing a day or night.

In fact, the moon, that bright heavenly body now so familiar to mankind that it is continually being visited and walked upon by earthlings, used to be an object of awe and mystery. It was blamed and credited for countless things, among them for having a powerful influence upon the weather.

Endless arguments went on about what caused a "wet moon" or a "dry moon." One faction maintained that when the first sliver of new moon appeared, if it was standing upright "the old Indian up there could hang up his powder horn and keep his powder dry," thus constituting a dry moon. Their opposite believers countered with the argument that with the moon in such a opsition "all the water would run out," and wet weather was imminent on earth. When the new moon lay on its back in the form of a bowl, they said, "the water was kept up there," and so the next week or so would be rainless. None of them suspected, of course, what now is common knowledge to nearly every school child: that the moon is a barren waste with no water up there at all.

"Thunder in the fall, no snow at all," used to be an old saying much used but also much laughed at by folks who lived in the Tug Hill area. They knew, as people still know, that a Tug Hill winter without snow, and plenty of it, was something that just didn't happen. But a certain part of the saying did hold true. A thunder storm in late fall still denotes a warm spell of weather to follow; just as one in early spring indicates a drop in the temperature with probably a snowfall following close behind.

In winter, a flaming red eastern sky in early morning usually meant that a storm was approaching, with unusually high winds. Strange to say, this rule did not hold true in summer.

Many an old-timer has been heard to say, "There's a wet spell comin', my j'ints are painin' me today." Or "Watch for a storm, my rheumatiz is actin' up." And as a usual thing, they would be right. What could cause this to be so? Atmospheric pressure? Humidity in the atmosphere?

When the air was said to be "hollow," transmitting minute sounds very clearly for long distances, it was an almost sure sign that a storm was approaching. In winter it would be snow, probably a blizzard . . . in summer, rain. When such a condition prevailed in the Redfield-

161

Osceola area in winter, folks used to say that it foretold a "Redfield thaw, three feet of snow."

On the opposite side of the scale, the presence of small whirlwinds or "dust devils" on a summer day predicted hot and dry weather to follow.

Old-time weather prophets derived many of their clues from watching the everyday behavior of animals, birds and insects. For instance, swallows and swifts flying very high forecast fair weather to come. In point of fact, they were of course only following the insects upon which they fed, so probably the flies and gnats were in on the secret too.

Gulls and other shore birds flying far inland indicated just the opposite. They seemed to sense when a marine disturbance with high winds was coming, and sought refuge away from the shorelines.

When "saw-whet owls," those minute members of the owl family that emitted a sound much like the filing of a saw, cried in the morning of a summer day, it was almost sure to rain before another twenty-four hours passed.

Farmyard hens that used to run loose around old-time farms, had their own special method of short-range weather predicting. If rain started to fall and all the hens made a dash for the nearest shelter, have no fear; the sun will soon be shining again. But on the other hand, if those same fowl oiled up their feathers and fared forth into the downpour to resume their usual activities, you might as well forget any outdoor jobs that you had planned for the rest of the day.

A horse yawning repeatedly and often also meant rain to come not later than the next day. This affect was no doubt caused by a high percentage of humidity and a low percentage of oxygen in the air; and often this "close" atmosphere affects humans the same way, especially asthma sufferers.

162

In summer, when a locust was heard to give his high-pitched, singing call, it inevitably meant that a long, hot, dry spell was to follow. This indication was always a welcome one with farmers who still had acres of hay to be gotten in. But on the other hand, when a clump of "rain-dancers," those small, mosquito-like insects that one often sees cavorting crazily a few feet above the ground, was observed in the evening, it meant that to-morrow was going to be a day to catch up on inside chores. Definitely, it would not be a hay-day.

And when that venerable old weather prophet, the robin, was seen perched on some high branch and "singing for rain," he usually had his request granted within a few hours.

And if the family cat was seen to be jumping and playing crazily for no apparent reason, he was said to be "wind crazy." Probably a modern scientist would say that this was caused by static electricity in the animal's fur. But to the old-time prognosticator it meant only one thing: high winds to follow.

Certain signs were eagerly watched for in the fall, by which the severity of the coming winter was evaluated. If wasps built their large, papery nests high above the ground, watch out for deep snow. If they were hung in low-growing bushes, the snow would be light and spotty. If muskrats built their houses high and massive, the winter would have much rain and high water; while a low house indicated little rain and much cold weather.

Even the lowly caterpillar was eagerly watched for the tell-tale colors of his winter coat. The black "fore and aft" sections indicated (supposedly) the comparative severity of the first and last parts of the coming winter. If the front black section was much longer than the back section, that meant that the more severe of the storms would come in the early part of the winter, with a midwinter lull indicated by the middle brown section,

163

and fewer storms at the close of the winter months. If the opposite coloration was present, then the weather prediction was also reversed. If the middle brown section was much longer than either black section, the winter would be warm and open, with little snow. But if both end sections were long black . . . wow. Better move to a warmer climate, for the winter would be one to remember for years to come.

Of course, everyone knows the myth of the woodchuck seeing, or not seeing, his shadow on Groundhog Day, February 2. In the Tug Hill area, most woodchucks are (sensibly) sound asleep under many feet of snow on that day. But the saying persists that IF the sun shines enough to project a shadow of His Woodchuckship, IF he wakes up and IF he cares to dig up through the deep drifts, he will immediately return to his cozy bed for six more weeks of sleep during six more weeks of winter weather.

Now it doesn't require a mathemetician to figure that whether or not the sun shines on that day, it will still be almost *seven* weeks before the start of spring about March the twenty-first. So it really makes little difference whether he does or doesn't.

Back in the days when most farmers butchered their own hogs, this work was usually done in late fall, when the weather was cold enough to preserve the meat for several days; and there was one weather indicator concealed inside the pig that winter prophets eagerly watched for and swore by. This was the long, narrow, liver-like gland attached to the stomach and known as the milt. If the forward end of this organ, nearest the stomach, was much thicker and broader, tapering off to a thin tail end, the winter would be rough and tough during the first months, and easier toward spring. If the condition of the milt was the opposite, so would the weather be. How a pigs' inner organs could be affected

164

by weather months ahead has never been satisfactorily explained to the author. But it is a fact that the belief was almost universal among country folk in the old days.

Perhaps a much more plausible indication of an impending winter was the fall crop of nuts, berries, and other storable edibles provided by Mother Nature for her wild creatures. A plentiful crop almost always indicated a hard winter ahead, while a scanty crop usually coincided with low-hung wasp nests and predominantly brown caterpillars.

In these days of scientific weather predicting with all the complicated equipment and systems available, such methods as the foregoing seem to most people to be very antiquated and unreliable. But they were all the old-timers had, and they served their purpose. A man swam or sank by his own judgment and knowledge. And certainly they did not cost the public the fabulous sums that are expended today by a munificent government to bring to them predictions of weather which is still whatever God chooses to make it.

THE BARE-FOOTED
BEAR TRAPPER

About the turn of the century, or a little before, conditions affecting the lives of the inhabitants of backwoods regions were vastly different from those of today. Life was much simpler and more self-contained than at the present time. No radio or television existed, and the few telephone lines extent were of necessity confined to the cities and heavily populated areas.

Only the richer of the population (and that almost always did not include backwoods dwellers) owned the new-fangled automobiles that could travel, it was rumored, up to thirty miles an hour on a good road; the latter being another commodity almost unheard of. Travel was confined almost exclusively to horse power, or in many cases the more primitive use of "shank's mare."

Families were larger, closer knit, and largely reliant upon themselves for the necessities and little luxuries of life. Everything that they had was either produced by themselves or wrested from the bountiful, but sometimes reluctant, hands of Nature. Fish and game were plentiful, but it took a considerable amount of know-how and ingenuity to convert them from the wild state to the dinner table.

Likewise, it required eternal vigilance on the part of the settlers to protect what their labors produced, from the depredations of some of Nature's bolder and more determined denizens. Bears, wolves, foxes, and an occasional panther were quick to take advantage of an un-

167

guarded moment to raid the bee-hives, dig up a potato patch, or make off with a choice hen, pig or sheep. Therefor, young boys growing up in this environment had to learn quickly and well to meet Nature on her own terms and to outwit her at every turn. Hunting, fishing and trapping were musts in every youth's education. Some learned better than others, and these were the ones who survived best.

Numbered among this select group were the Caster boys: "Billie Ward," the eldest of the family, and Percy, who was the youngest boy. Billie Ward became famous as a hunter, guide and raconteur; living his life out as a bachelor, footloose and devoid of marital ties to restrict him in his favorite pursuits. Percy, who later earned the sobriquet of "Beartrap," is still hale and active at seventy-odd years, and is recognized as one of the best trout fishermen in the Tug Hill area. It is with one of his early experiences that this tale is concerned.

The Caster boys' father was a farmer in the northern end of Redfield township, an area that even today is semi-backwoods and plenty wild. At that time it was plagued with an abundance of bears that made nuisances of themselves by robbing beehives and raiding pig-pens and flocks of sheep. It was a well-known fact that a bear that had tasted mutton was never again content with conventional bruin fare; so once started, they kept on killing and killing.

These beasts were hunted down and exterminated by irate farmers in any manner possible, and at any time of year. However, there was one old veteran who had angered the farmers for years, and who had proved to be too wily to succumb to even their most expert methods. Traps, dogs, poison, and ambushes had all been tried and proven to be of no avail. And still his raids went on from spring to fall.

Like most farmers in the region, the elder Mr. Caster

168

kept a large flock of sheep, both for their fleece, which provided a source of extra income, and their flesh, which was in those days a staple ingredient of rural diet. And like the rest, his flock was periodically raided by the cagey old master of sheep killing. During the spring and early summer of the year in question his forays had accounted for nine of the Caster woolies, and young Percy determined to put an end to all this.

Procuring a large and heavy bear trap, he carried it to the site of the last slaughter, at a point hidden from the house by a slight ridge and about half a mile away. It was mid-summer and Percy, in his early teens, had been going barefoot for months, as was the custom for boys in the early times. But even though his feet were tough and horny from constant contact with stones and briers, this made it rather difficult to set the cumbersome trap. However, it was accomplished, and securely chained to a heavy hardwood drag, it was carefully concealed and baited with the remains of the bear's latest kill, which was wired to a tree high above the ground. The boy hoped that this would bring satisfactory results.

For almost a week he attended the trap faithfully morning and night with no results. During this time the bait became increasingly ripe and smelly, and it was probably this effluvium that reminded the bear that he had left something behind, and caused him to go back after it. Anyway, it was this decision that turned the tide against him.

As he checked the trap site early one morning, young Percy suddenly became aware that the place was pretty badly torn up and the trap and clog were gone. Now, the boy carried no gun, being armed only with a short-handled axe, but nevertheless he began to cautiously follow the trail of uprooted brush and chewed saplings. This led into a thick, swampy area, from which came only ominous silence. Try as he would, Percy could not hear a sound. This seemed strange to him, as he knew that trapped bears usually put up a devil of a fuss. Maybe the old fellow had pulled loose from the trap and was long gone. And again, perhaps he was just lying low, waiting for the boy to get within easy distance for an attack. Percy had no misconceptions concerning the dangerous proclivities of a trapped or wounded bear. Grasping his axe a little tighter, he pressed on.

Suddenly, from behind an old windfall in which the trap clog had become entangled, there rose up a bellowing black apparition that seemed to be composed entirely of evilly gleaming eyes, red snarling jaws, and slashing claws that looked to the startled boy to be six inches long. The sight stopped Percy in his tracks — in fact, it reversed those tracks completely and increased the tempo at which he had been making them by about ten-fold. Before he realized it he was halfway home, running hard and still clutching his axe. Breathless, and with his bare feet scarcely touching the ground, he burst into the barn where his older brother Clyde was working..

"I've got the bear," he shouted. "I've got the bear."

After he had calmed down enough to talk coherently, Percy related what had happened. It was decided that only Billie Ward, who was older and more experienced, was competent to handle the situation properly; but he was at work in a nearby sawmill belonging to Arthur Yerdon, so it was further decided not to bother him. Percy and Clyde (who had no interest in hunting and was unskilled in the use of firearms) decided that they could handle the matter alone, so they armed themselves and started out. Clyde carried a razor-sharp double-bitted axe, and young Percy lugged a big old 38-40 Winchester rifle, his pockets sagging with no less than sixty rounds of ammunition. In his excitement, the boys' bare

170

feet seemed impervious to the stones and splinters that they encountered along the way.

When they reached the spot where the bear had been hung up, they found that he had disentangled himself and gone on deeper into the swamp. Slowly and carefully they followed the trail of chewed and clawed brush, Percy and the Winchester in the lead. Danger they knew there was. A trapped or wounded bear will often lie quietly in wait until his pursuers are within easy striking distance, and the boys knew this. Slower and slower grew the pace, until Clyde began to grow impatient.

"Hurry up Perce, or we'll be all day," he urged.

"Well, if you're in sucha big hurry, why don't you get up here ahead?" returned Percy. So Clyde and his axe went ahead, but at no increase in speed.

About three-quarters of a mile from where he had been trapped, the old sheep-killer finally came to the end of the trail. There the boys found him firmly anchored in a clump of alders, foam-slavered jaws snarling defiance.

"There he is, Perce, give it to him," yelled Clyde.

Percy warily circled the old killer, searching for an opening for a good shot. Of course he had no way of knowing if the animal was firmly anchored, or if he might come charging out at them at any moment. Presently he was able to get a fairly clear view of the bear's head, and, taking quick aim, he let go a shot. The bullet sped true to the spot between the eyes, and the big bruin's sheep-killing days were over. Even then young Percy was not satisfied and fired another shot into the neck for good measure.

When they considered it safe to do so, the boys warily approached to look at their prize, and it was then that they received a real shock. The foot that was caught in the trap was almost completely severed, hanging only by a few frayed shreds of flesh and sinew. Had the animal made a last determined effort he might have found himself free to attack his hunters, and in that case the story might have had an entirely different ending.

After the big bruin had been transported to the barn by stoneboat and hung up in an apple tree, farmers from far and near came to look it over. It was determined by a deformity of a hind foot that this was, indeed, the old outlaw who had caused them so much woe and expense. Percy reeived a lot of praise from the veteran bear hunters who had done their best to bring him to account and failed. May it not be construed as a pun when it was said that there were many sheepish faces among them, then and whenever the bare-footed bear trapper was mentioned.

VIGNETTES

In the process of researching for the bigger and more important anecdotes concerning any given region, one invariably comes across many seemingly insignificant facts and happenings which, nevertheless, titillate a fleeting interest. This may be because of their humor, their drama, or some unique quality or circumstance that they may portray.

Whatever the cause of their interest, every researcher probably collects a large store of these little sidelights that never reach the general public, even though many of the public would no doubt enjoy them quite as much as the researcher. Here are a few dug up while snooping into the past history of the Tug Hill territory.

Hough's Cave

High up on the eastern flank of Tug Hill, two or three miles south of Martinsburg and near what is now Route 12D, there stands a state historical marker designating the site of the once famous Hough's Cave.

Nothing much now remains to be seen there. The cave's entrance, only a few feet from the heavily traveled highway, slopes downward from the level expanse of a cow-pasture, and has been almost completely filled with field stones and rubbish. The giant elm that used to stand like a sentinel near its entrance, and could easily be seen both from "the loved hills of Martinsburg" and from the higher reaches of Tug Hill to the south, is long gone. Only its low-cut stump remains.

But legend has it that this cave was at one time a cool

173

and comforting haven of safety for many a band of black fugitives fleeing to Canada from the plantations of the southern states. Roomy and well ventilated, it provided an ideal spot for them to rest up and enjoy the food that had been smuggled in by the local abolitionists.

It is said that this cavern once contained a vast pool of pure spring water, suitable for either drinking or bathing purposes. Probably this water has soothed many a pair of feet, sore and aching from stumbling over the rocky terrain, usually in the darkness of night.

Certainly Hough's Cave was no scintillating playground for thousands of sightseers, like Mammoth Cave or Carlsbad Caverns. But assuredly it received the blessings of many a transient on the famous Underground Railroad.

* * * * *

A Pail of Water

Sheridan "Sherd" Cross was a descendant of one of the first pioneers in the Town of Orwell. His father, Palmer Cross, moved while a young man to the Town of Sandy Creek, and there young Sherd was brought up. The writer first made his acquaintance when he was well past middle age; a large, florid-faced bachelor who had devoted most of his adult years to the lumbering industry. In later life he settled down on a little fertile farm near Lacona and spent his time raising chickens, garden produce, and several kinds of berries. An inveterate story teller, he was always good for an hour's entertainment once he got started.

A very amusing story was told about Sherd in his younger days. It seems that he and his father, both being of the same temperamental makeup, did not get along well at all. The young man had often, in times of family arguments, voiced his intention of leaving home to seek his fortune.

174

However, he had never carried out his threat, until one day when the bickering had been a little more intense than usual, and bitter words had been said. On this day, Sherd's mother handed him a water pail and asked him to go out to the pump for a pail of water. The young man took the pail and went outside, slamming the door shut behind him.

After considerable time had passed and the desired pail of water was not forthcoming, the mother went to the door to see what was keeping her son. There on the doorstep sat the pail of water, but young Sherd had disappeared. And that was the last they saw of him for eleven long years.

It later developed that during that time he had made his way to the lumbering woods of Michigan and Wisconsin, where he had worked as lumberjack and riverdriver; going from job to job as necessity or whimsey dictated, and gaining a vast knowledge of the industry.

It may be that after eleven years he felt that he had established beyond a doubt his independence and ability to take care of himself. Perhaps he had seen enough of the wandering life and wished for something a little less adventuresome but more assured. Or maybe he was smitten with plain, old-fashioned homesickness. Anyway, he came back to his parents and the old home place.

History does not tell just how he accomplished this, but it may be safely assumed that he rode the rails into Lacona, and from there walked the three or four miles to his old home. As he came into the dooryard, almost eleven years to the day from the time when he had left it, no one was in sight. But there on the well-curb sat an empty pail. Picking it up, Sherd pumped it full of water, and with it in his hand went and knocked on the kitchen door. His mother opened the door, and a look of joyous surprise came over her lined old face.

"Why son, it's you," she cried incredulously.

"Yes Ma, it's me," replied Sherd. "And say, Ma, here's your pail of water."

* * * * *

Ask a Silly Question ...

One time Percy "Beartrap" Caster and his wife were visiting the Sandy Creek Fair, when they happened by a concession that was selling tombstones. They stopped to examine the stones, and immediately a high-pressure salesman spotted them and started giving them a sales-pitch. Percy didn't let him go on for long.

"Why, we're way ahead of you," he said. "We've had our stone bought and set for over ten years now."

"Was it one of our stones?" the salesman asked.

"Sure was," agreed Percy.

"Well good," enthused the salesman. "Tell me, how do you like it?"

"Don't know," came back Percy. "We ain't used it yet."

* * * * *

The Rose Grotto of Lewisburg

One of the most unusual discoveries in the history of American mining came to light one day during the routine operation of a limestone quarry near the now defunct village of Lewisburg, in Lewis County. This location was rather on the northwest boundary of the Tug Hill plateau, and is now included in the sprawling reaches of the giant military reservation known as Camp Drum.

The quarry was originally opened to supply lime rock to the kilns from which came the lime used in the production of iron in the surrounding iron mills. At one time it furnished work for a sizable crew of men, but as

176

the surrounding iron deposits were used up the industry gradually died out. Today, the quarry is filled with water, and is rarely visited because of its location within the confines of Camp Drum.

One day early in the autumn of 1906, workers loading the tramcars with rock in the quarry were startled to hear the dreaded grating sound of a rock-slide behind and above them. Shouting a warning, the whole crew scrambled to safety before the tumbling rocks reached them.

Somewhat unnerved by their close call, they were resting from their exertions when one man noticed a hole in the side of the cliff uncovered by the slide. This had not been there before, nor had they ever encountered anything like it.

With his curiosity somewhat piqued by his discovery, this man finally decided to investigate farther. Gingerly making his way upward over the loose and treacherous rock, he inched his way along until he was on a level with the opening, about forty feet below the top of the quarry wall. Suddenly he stopped short, transfixed and speechless at the unutterable beauty of the scene before him.

From the opening, which was about four feet square at the front, blinding rays of rose and violet light were reflected outward from the giant crystals within as the sunlight beat upon them. Shading his eyes, the man saw that the opening enlarged into a room about five feet high and ten feet wide, and extended for twenty feet or more into the living rock. The walls and floor of the cavern were virtually lined with these large, smooth crystals, and the floor was scattered with them. Measuring them with his eye he saw that some of them were more than three feet square, and weighed, he estimated, up to one thousand pounds each. The whole interior of the grotto was bathed by an intermingling of rose and amethyst light as these huge jewels reflected the unfamiliar light of the sun.

Beckoning to his companions below, the man summoned them to view the awesome sight. After talking it over, they decided that such an unusualy discovery should be brought to the attention of the quarry foreman. He was summoned, and in turn was dumbfounded by the unusual beauty of the strange formations. A Miss Sterling, who was one of the owners of the quarry, was notified, and she decided that the cavern should be left undisturbed until it could be examined by a geologist from the State Department of Mines.

This official was amazed at the perfect formation of the cave's crystals, and suggested to his superiors that they should be transferred to a State museum in Albany, where they could be displayed in an appropriate manner for the appreciation of the public.

The plan was agreed upon, and the crystals were carefully removed. Measurements were taken and an elaborate plan of the cavern's interior was prepared and used in the creation of an exact reproduction of the grotto in the musuem. Altogether, about fourteen tons of material were transported and used.

It was theorized that this beautiful opening in the living rock had lain undiscovered for aeons of time since its creation by some unknown means. After thorough chemical tests of the materials had been made, a highly scientific explanation of the formation of the crystals, isolated as they were from all influence of outside atmosphere, was made for the edification of the scientific-minded. However, the layman can view for himself the amazing beauty of the scintillating grotto discovered by accident in the old White Rock quarry at Lewisburg.

A River of Salmon

In pioneer days those who settled in Jefferson and Oswego counties early discovered that streams flowing into Lake Ontario contained an abundance of salmon, and these delicious fish formed a welcome addition to the simple diet of the early settlers.

Salmon River, in particular, was well supplied with fish, and was without a doubt a favorite fishing place for the Indians before the advent of white men. When a run was on great shoals of salmon went up the river, thousands at a time, their fins breaking above the water and flashing like floating silver in the sunlight.

The annual fishing expeditions engaged in by the men of the families must have been long anticipated and well remembered occasions, especially by the younger members of the parties. An old newspaper account states that the Lilleys, one of the families that settled on the banks of Deer Creek in the early days, speared so many salmon that it took an ox to bring them home.

Although the fish could be speared in the daytime, night was the favorite time, and by the aid of a boat and a plentiful supply of pine knots for a jack-light, a great many fish could be secured.

In Evart's *History of Oswego County* it is related how one man speared sixty-three salmon during the burning of one jack-light of pine knots, calculated to have burned for about seventeen minutes. He and a companion captured two hundred and thirty during the four hours between dark and midnight; and one hundred of these, taken at random from the pile, weighed fourteen hundred and seventy-five pounds.

Many have heard their grandparents tell of the days when the salmon came up the stream in such large numbers that coming to Salmon River Falls and being, of course, unable to leap the obstruction (one hundred eighteen feet) they became so thickly packed in the pool at the foot of the falls that their backs showed above the water, and many were continually being pushed out onto the banks.

It is even told that one man actually walked across the pool on solid fish; but this, of course, is another of the tall tales so rampant in the old days.

* * * * *

The Utica-Sackets Harbor Stage Route

The old stagecoach line between Utica and Sackets Harbor was listed as being eighty-three miles in length, and on this route were located sixteen inns, taverns, and stage-houses where travelers could obtain food and drink, and tired horses could be exchanged for fresh ones.

This would average only slightly over five miles between stops, which in this day and age seems a ridiculously short distance. But a mile was really a mile in one of those cumbersome, swaying, rough-riding old stagecoaches; hard on travelers and horses alike. In spring and fall most of the roads were composed of mud and boulders, and in the dry weather of summer of boulders and dust. Often progress was restricted to one or two miles an hour, and in these stretches even a five-mile trip could become irksome and make the sight of a rest-stop welcome indeed.

According to the Farmer's Calendar or Utica Almanac for the year 1816, the first tavern was Spencer's at Deerfield, only one mile out of Utica. But then came a long but comparatively easy stretch to Trenton, where Ives' stagehouse was located and fresh horses were obtained. This was the longest single distance on the route without a tavern or rest stop of any kind.

Five miles beyond that was the Hough Tavern at

180

Remsen, and after that there was a thirteen-mile distance to Boonville, but with the Sheldon and Deming taverns located midway. At Boonville was Snow's stagehouse; at Leyden, four miles farther on, was Starr's stagehouse; and at Turin, three miles distance, was Dodd's stagehouse.

Between Turin and Martinsburg, a distance of twelve miles, no towns were listed, but halfway between was a stagehouse kept by a Mr. House. Lee's stagehouse was located at Martinsburg, Wehle's at Lowville, four miles away; Dickerson's at Denmark, eight miles beyond; and Moseley's at Champion, seven miles from Denmark. Cole and Colton's tavern was in Rutland, six miles farther, and in Watertown was another Lee's stagehouse.

At Brownville, the last town before Sackets Harbor was reached, was Joy's stagehouse. And as the stage pulled into the terminal at Sackets, those who had made the full trip must have felt a wonderful sense of achievement at having lasted the entire distance.

* * * * *

The Hanchett Tavern

The Hanchett Tavern was at one time one of the most famed hostelries of the whole northern country. Built in 1840 by John Tifft, it was located at the intersection of the North Ridge Road and the Salt Road , (now U.S. Route 11) and stood facing the latter, in an easterly direction.

Nearby were several houses and a store, a schoolhouse, and a blacksmith shop. In later years the store was also converted into a dwelling by a Mr. Waterman Brown.

About 1847, Mr. Tifft sold the tavern to Silas Hanchett, whose ancestry could be traced directly back to

181

William the Conqueror, in the year 1080. Apparently, he was the son-in-law of the original owner, as he had married Mahala Tifft in 1826, away back in the days when knee-breeches and buckles, silk hats, ruffles, and brocaded waistcoats were the fashion. He was one of the real old-time genial, hospitable hosts. It was his custom to sit at the head of the table at mealtime and do the serving, and it was said that in addition to excellent victuals, he also served up a brand of witty and sparkling repartee that kept his guests amused and happy.

In the days before a railroad invaded the region, the tavern was a stage stop, where passengers could obtain food and liquid refreshment, and fresh horses were kept for the vehicles.

According to all accounts, the tavern was a very beautiful building when in its heyday. The large part of the house, rectangular in shape, had three rooms in front on the ground floor, one of these being the bar-room, in which stood a huge oak bar. At one end of this was a large earthen jar with a spigot, kept full of ice-water at all times.

The other large room was the public sitting-room, which required forty yards of rag carpeting a yard wide to cover its floor. The front hall connected with a smaller private parlor for the use of the family. The hall had a staircase with a landing, leading up to the second floor, which contained the ballroom extending the entire length of the building, with a seat running all around the sides. This room was sufficiently large to have seven square dance sets in progress at the same time.

Up in one end of the room there had been built into the wall what was known as a sounding bottle. This was a very large bottle with its mouth just inside the room, the rest sunk into the wall. The device was supposed to absorb the vibrations of dancing feet, and greatly improve the acoustics inside the room. The musicians' stand was in the center of the rear wall, where the players of the violins, the bass viol, and the other instruments sat with the conductor and the square dance caller. Hanging from the rail around the musicians' stand were old-fashioned glazed chintz curtains.

Light was furnished by candle-holders which hung at intervals around the room, each containing two large candles and furnished with a large, bright tin reflector, about the size of a dinner plate. The walls were painted and had a stenciled border all around. Back of the ballroom were seven sleeping rooms.

Back of the main or upright part of the house was a large wing which extended west, with two doors, one from the bar-room and one from the public sitting room. In this wing was a large dining room with a very high ceiling. In one corner was a trapdoor which went down into the cellar. When banquets were held in this room, over a hundred people could be seated at tables at one time.

Off the dining room were two more bedrooms, and the old-fashioned buttery where milk and other articles of food were kept, as well as the dishes. Adjoining this room and running toward the south was a long wing with another entry connecting, which had an old-fashioned pantry containing all the kitchen utensils. On the other side was a very large kitchen.

Occupying nearly all of the south side of this kitchen was a huge old fireplace with all the cranes and other appurtenances necessary for the fireplace cookery of those early days. Beside it was a large brick oven for doing the stupendous amount of baking required. On the other side of the fireplace, built in with stone, was a huge iron kettle used to heat the water needed for doing the housework. In front of the hearth were large flagstones. The kitchen was ceiled, and like all the other rooms in the house, had old-fashioned chair rails.

183

From the kitchen a door opened into the rest of the wing, which was occupied by the woodshed, where over a hundred cords of sawed wood could be stored. Adjoining this was the ice house, in which they could place enough ice to last throughout the entire year. This was stored in winter and carefully packed with sawdust to keep it from the air.

Outside the kitchen and dining room was a little yard enclosed by a picket fence, and just a little way from that was the old pump from which many neighbors drew their drinking water, and where the horses that went by were stopped to be watered.

A little north of the tavern was a long shed with a rack running along its rear side, where hay and grain could be placed for the horses after they had been driven in. Connecting with this was the large barn, the doors of which were wide enough to allow four horses to be driven through abreast. There were stalls, both single and double, at each side, and the rear of the barn was partitioned off for the use of cattle.

When the stage-coaches were coming from the north or south, the drivers would blow their horns to warn of their approach, usually about half a mile away. The coaches would drive up to the door with a great deal of noise and clamor, the driver cracking his long whip over the back of the horses. Very often the coaches were drawn by four horses, one team hitched ahead of the other. The luggage of the passengers was carried in racks on the top and back of the vehicle. It was always a moment of great excitement for those in the tavern when the stage came in.

The old inn, steeped in all its traditions of jolly times and old-time hospitality, was destroyed by fire many years ago, along with all its furnishings and records. Fire in the chimney of the house across the road caused sparks to fall upon the roof of the inn; and as it was built mostly of pine well dried out by many years of use, it burned like tinder. Today, not a trace remains of the famous old Hanchett's Tavern.

* * * * *

The Founder of Arbor Day

Arbor Day was an occasion much looked forward to in bygone days by most school children in the North Country. It was on this one day of the school year that they enjoyed a let-down in the rigid routine of learning, and were allowed to gambol in the outdoors to their hearts' content, without the necessity of playing hookey.

Usually on Arbor Day studies were restricted to a very perfunctory one hour (or less) in the morning. Then, especially in the rural schools, the whole student body was released outside to rake and generally clean up the school grounds. After that the ritual of planting flowers and at least one tree was gone through, this supposedly being the high point of the day.

But what really constituted the day's high point was the field trip after lunch. Dressed in rough and sturdy clothing brought along purposely for the trip, the boys and girls were free, under a teacher's guidance of course, to wander and ramble through the woods and fields for the purpose of studying nature. Although some studying was done, in all fairness it must be confessed that most of the afternoon was devoted to the playing of pranks, especially by the boys. A good deal of slingshot practice could be gotten in, and even a little fishing if a fellow had the foresight to bring along a hook and line.

Although Arbor Day is not what it used to be, it is still recognized in most of the states. It was first established by the then-acting governor of Nebraska, who introduced the following resolution:

RESOLVED: That Wednesday, the 10th day of

185

April, 1872, be especially set apart and consecrated for tree planting in the State of Nebraska; and that the State Board of Agriculture hereby name it Arbor Day.

The resolution was adopted in Nebraska, and the idea was gradually copied by the other states.

All of this, of course, is general knowledge. What is not generally known is that the founder, J. Sterling Morton, was born in the little village of Adams, N.Y., and spent his early boyhood years there. The rock-ribbed environment during his beginning years may have helped to instill in him the sturdiness of character that sustained him through a long and somewhat stormy political career, which finally placed him in the high position of Secretary of Agriculture in the cabinet of President Cleveland.

While he was quite young, his parents, grandfather, and uncle all moved to Monroe, Michigan, where the grandfather and uncle founded and published a newspaper. Previously the grandfather had published papers in Adams and Watertown, and the inherited newsman instinct in young J. Sterling probably influenced him in the founding of literary publications in two colleges. It also caused him to be expelled from the University of Michigan where his "University Magazine," the first to be published on that campus, championed the cause of an ousted faculty member. That event, coming just before his graduation, engendered a sense of rancor against the University that he never forgot.

Shortly after leaving college, albeit forcibly, he married a girl whom he had known while a student in Wesleyan Seminary, and the newlyweds immediately departed for St. Louis. From there they went to Bellevue, in the budding state of Nebraska. There Morton also became a crusading newspaper man, and rose quickly in politics to become president of the Nebraska State

186

Board of Agriculture. From there he went on to become acting governor in 1866; and finally to the post of Secretary of Agriculture in 1893. Ironically, he was picked for this post by a President whose candidacy he had bitterly opposed.

Probably the proliferous forests around his old home on the flank of Tug Hill had left a lasting impression on him. After going to Nebraska, he was quick to notice the comparative scarcity of trees in that state, and decided to try to do something about it. His contention was that if every citizen of Nebraska planted one tree on one day of each year, the state would soon show a decided increase in shade and ornamental trees, as well as forest resources. That is said to have been the moving factor in his resolution while acting governor that created Arbor Day, "consecrated for tree planting."

Mortons' old home in Adams is said to have been moved to make room for the expansion of the cemetery on the hill at the south edge of the village.

* * * * *

Restless Spirits

Like almost any other area, the Tug Hill region had its tales of ghostly visitations and haunted places. Many of these have been lost, but a few still remain.

Typical of these is the one about the lady who used to live near Lowville, whose husband was an inveterate gambler. Try as she might to break him of the habit of indulging in occasional poker parties with a few of his cronies, all her preaching was in vain.

"My card playing is harmless and dont' hurt no one," he used to argue.

"But I'm going to break you of your sinful gambling if it's the last thing I ever do, Matt," she would tell her husband.

In this boast she did not make good in life, as he was still a confirmed gambler at the time of her death. But so great was her determination that she went right on with her efforts even after she was dead and buried.

At first it appeared that she had failed dismally. With his house now womanless, Matt converted it into a gambling headquarters where more and larger poker games took place. But after a while he began to notice that one by one his former cronies stopped coming to his place, and even commenced to avoid him in public. The games grew less and less frequent and soon died out altogether due to lack of players. This puzzled him, so one day he cornered one of his former visitors and began to question him.

At first the man acted cagey and unwilling to talk, but after persistent questioning he finally told a strange story.

"One night I was on my way home after a game at your house," he related, "and when I was passing that swamp just this side of your place, all at once there was your wife, walking right along beside me. She looked all sort of light and shimmery, but she could talk — man, how she could talk! She told me all about the error of my ways in keeping on gambling instead of staying home with my family, and warned me that something terrible would happen if I kept it up. When she'd had her say she just disappeared, and I took off for home. Ain't touched a card since, and I sure ain't going to, either."

One by one, the wayward husband questioned all his former cronies, and found out that his erstwhile spouse had indeed been very busy. The same experience had befallen each and every one of them. All had taken her at her ghostly word and decided to swear off poker playing, and they all urged him to do the same.

After giving the matter due thought, he decided that this was the best thing to do. After all, he reasoned, if his

188

wife had been so dedicated to breaking him of gambling that she continued her efforts from the grave, even to the point of depriving him of friends with whom to play, she must have had a very good reason, and the least he could do would be to honor her wishes. So he swore off card playing, and after that the visitations stopped.

* * * * *

Then of course there was the ghost of the murdered pack-peddler who used to stalk along the Old State Road where it passed through Dead Man's Hollow, near Redfield. This one never spoke to anyone, and the nearest he ever came to doing any harm was to scare those who saw him half out of their wits.

* * * * *

And there is the story of the ghost of Dr. Samuel Guthrie who used to appear in the house in which he lived for many years in Sackets Harbor.

Dr. Guthrie was, of course, a rather famous personage. During the war of 1812 he was a surgeon for the American forces, and in addition to his propensities as a doctor, he possessed an intensely inventive turn of mind. He it was who perfected and patented the percussion cap, which practically revolutionized the use of muzzle-loading firearms, especially in wet weather. And even more important, in 1831 he developed the formula for the manufacture of chloroform, which could lull a patient into merciful and harmless unconsciousness while a painful operation was taking place.

Dr. Guthrie died in 1848, and his house in Sackets Harbor naturally passed into the hands of other owners. It was not until many years after his death that any spiritual manifestations were noticed there. The first of these was a rattling, as of bones, in a closet where the doctor had kept his skeletons (literally speaking).

189

Then one night a young boy sleeping in an upstairs room of the house suddenly called to his mother. When she appeared at his bedroom door, he asked her:

"Who was that old man who was just standing where you are, looking in at me?"

"You were dreaming. Go back to sleep now," the mother said, trying to calm his fears.

"No, I wasn't asleep," the boy insisted. "He had a long beard and a tall hat, and I could see the stair rail right through him."

On the evening when the grandfather of the famliy who occupied the house lay dying, his wife remained in the room with him, trying to ease the hard passage by her presence. As she leaned upon the foot of the bed, her gaze intent upon the pale face of her husband, suddenly she sensed that they were not alone in the room.

Glancing to the side she saw a white-haired old gentleman bending over the bed staring at the sick man. This figure was dressed in a fashion long out of date. No doors had opened or closed in the room and his sudden appearance startled the lady, but she immediately recognized him as Dr. Guthrie from pictures she had seen of him.

This proved too much for the over-wrought woman, and she slumped to the floor in a faint. When she was found and revived some time later, there was no sign of the ghostly visitor; but her husband had passed peacefully away. And although there was no chloroform in the house, nor had there been any for many years, still the room reeked of the odor of the anesthetic.

One wonders: did compassion and the natural instincts of the physician compel the good doctor to return to ease the passage of a human soul, with the agent of mercy that he had been instrumental in bringing into being?

190

Quite often military posts have haunts, and old Fort Ontario at Oswego is no exception. In fact, this post used to have two of them.

The first, in point of seniority at least, dated back to Revolutionary times, as he wore the white breeches, scarlet coat, and crossed belts of the British regular soldier. He was known rather affectionately as George Fykes. Whether or not this was really the name of the corporeal owner of the spirit is not known, but the tombstone of a British soldier by that name may be seen in the post cemetery.

For a century or more George made at least one visitation to each new garrison at the Fort, some one of which would get a chill from seeing him wandering around, mumbling to himself. But no one ever took him very seriously, and apparently he has given up whatever purpose he had, as no one has seen him since before World War II.

The second haunt at the Fort was more cagey and did not appear in bodily form. This one made itself manifest in the form of a small round light, about the size of a saucer, that hovered above the head of the guard walking a certain post.

According to a soldier who was stationed there about 1920, the first guard to notice this phenomena thought that some of his friends were playing a trick on him, and decided not to mention it to his superior officer. But the next night the guard on that post noticed the light and mentioned it to the other man, who was his friend. Upon comparing notes they decided that they were being made the butt of a practical joke, and agreed that they would handle the matter in their own way and turn the tables on the jokesters. So the next night that one of them was assigned to the post, one of them hid in a nearby vantage point to watch, while the other walked sentry duty.

Promptly at midnight the light appeared above the

pacing guard's head and proceeded to keep pace with him. From his vantage point the watcher could see that no human agency could possibly produce such an effect by any known means, so it was decided that this must be the spirit of some long-departed guard who had once walked that same post, and for some unknown reason had returned to do ghostly duty there again.

The word spread throughout the Fort, and soon many men began to object to doing night duty at that particular post. It became so bad that a board of officers was convened to make an investigation of the matter, but after listening to the testimony of several witnesses who had been disturbed by the phenomena, no explanation of it could be arrived at.

So no one ever knew just who or what the second haunt was, but since the Fort has been restored as a national monument, no sign of the mysterious light has been seen.

* * * * *

Works of Art

Most of the old settlers possessed a keen sense of humor. Without it, at times it would have been very dif ficult to get through certain situations, even as today. Some of them possessed a sense of logic, which also made life a little easier. Surely Jay Barnes, whose antics and foibles were chronicled in "Tug Hill Country," could lay claim to both of these assets.

Mr. Barnes was a tin peddler by trade, spending most of his time during spring, summer and fall driving a jangling tin-cart along the country roads of the North Country. But he also owned a small farm at the foot of the Wheat Hill, on the Lacona-Smartville road, where he spent his winters and between trips lay-overs. This he worked at sporadically; but essentially he was a trav-

192

eling man, and when spring came and the open road began to beckon, his farming was rather neglected until late fall.

On one of those times that he was home in early spring, he was one day sharpening fence posts near the highway when along came Thomas Hamer, who lived a couple of miles farther up the road. Of course. Mr. Hamer stopped his rig to visit for a while, and during the course of the conversation he remarked on the fine job Jay was doing sharpening the fence-posts. His pride overcoming his modesty, Jay readily agreed with him.

"Yes sir, the work of an expert," Mr. Hamer commented. "It seems too bad to bury such fine workmanship in the ground." And Jay agreed with him.

After they had talked for a while, Mr. Hamer drove on toward home and completely forgot the conversation until a week or so later when he was again passing the Barnes residence. There, neatly set in a row that would become a road-fence, were the fence-posts in question. But instead of being set in the cenventional manner, these were reversed, with their tops set into the ground and their finely-hewed bottoms pointing proudly toward the heavens — up where everyone could see and admire the work of a master craftsman.

*   *   *   *   *

The Montague Prison Camp

Lewis County pioneered an unique experiment in penal management when, in 1936, they established a prison camp near Parkers, designed to accommodate the overflow from the county jail at Lowville. This institution was overcrowded due to the great increase of arrests for minor offenses, brought on by the social imbalance and the extreme indigence suffered by some during the depression years.

The pattern for the experiment was set by the State of New York when, in 1930, they established a similar camp near Number Four, to accommodate an overflow of inmates at Great Meadow Prison, near Comstock. These prisoners were sent to the camp to be used in the construction of a road, and were dealt with mostly on the honor basis. Unfortunately, the honor of one convict was not quite equal to his dislike for penal servitude, with the result that he ran away at the first opportunity. But he was soon captured, and in the fall the whole kit and kaboodle of them were shipped back to Great Meadow.

But Lewis County Judge Miller B. Moran thought that the idea was basically workable, and late in 1935 he asked the Board of Supervisors for permission to institute such a program. Permission was granted, and in the spring of 1936 the camp was built on the Flat Rock Road, about one-half mile west of Parkers, in the Town of Montague. About twenty minor offenders from the county jail were lodged there under the management of Morris Bedford, of New Bremen. Sheriff Albert Schoff organized a wood cutting program, and several thousand cords of stove-wood were produced during the next four years.

During the summer months a large garden project was also conducted here, and many bushels of potatoes, as well as great quantities of other vegetables were produced each year. These garden products took care of the needs of the camp, and the surplus was used by the welfare department of the county.

Being, as they were, short-term offenders, personnel at the camp was necessarily fluid. No one stayed there long, but some enjoyed the experience and believed that they were benefitted by it. Altogether, the experiment was considered to be very worthwhile, and was later copied by at least one other county.

194

Two other deputies, Royal Hill and William Tompkins, later served as managers of the camp. The program ended on December 31, 1940, when only two prisoners were available for residency there. The property was later sold to private owners, and the old prison camp now houses members of a sportsmens' club.

* * * * *

No Screened Air for Him

Clyde Caster was a bachelor who lived alone some years ago in a small house about four miles east of Lacona, up in the Boyston hills. He was an expert blacksmith who made his living working at his trade in a shop near his home. Clyde was slightly eccentric in some of his ways, just as most of us are, but some who did not know him well considered him to be a fool because of his eccentricities. However, a few of them who tried to take advantage of him, or badger him for amusement purposes, soon learned that this was not so.

A classic example of this occurred one day when a Lacona store keeper, intent upon amusing some of his friends who happened to be in the store, saw Clyde approaching upon the sidewalk.

"Want to see some fun?" he asked, and upon their assent he stepped to the door and accosted Clyde.

"Come in here a minute, Clyde," he requested, "I've got something to show you."

Clyde readily entered the store, carrying the old feed bag that he used to tote groceries home rolled up under his arm.

"Whatcha got?" he queried.

"Well sir," said the storekeeper, "see that clock right there That clock will run nine days without winding. What do you think of that?"

"Hmm, quite a thing," said Clyde musingly. "Wonder how long it'd run if you *did* wind it?"

It is said that the merchant's friends did not let him forget the episode for many a year.

One of Clyde's aversions was the wearing of new looking clothing. Upon buying a new pair of pants he would immediately sew patches on the areas most exposed to wear, sometimes using white twine for the purpose, This, he said, prolonged the life of the original garment.

One time his younger brother, Percy, tired of seeing Clyde going about in patches, presented him with a new pair of pants. A few days later he encountered Clyde wearing the same old pants, but with new patches.

"Where are those new pants I gave you?" asked Percy.

"Oh, I cut them up for patches," answered Clyde nonchalantly.

Another of Clyde's bachelor dislikes was having screens on windows and doors. Once each year his sister would visit him for a week, during which time she would give his house a thorough cleaning. Before she left she would tack new screens over the windows and see that the screen door was repaired. But hardly would she be gone before Clyde would remove the window screens, and prop the screen door wide open. One day someone asked him why he did this.

"Well, I'll tell you," replied Clyde. "I just don't like to breathe screened air."

*　　*　　*　　*　　*

The Boylston Meteor

Many years ago the scientific world was set agog by the news that a giant meteor had fallen in the wilds of Boylston. This report, later proved to be a hoax, was attributed to one Chet Hull, an Oswego newspaper man, who originated it as a practical joke. If this were so, the

196

results must have surpassed his wildest dreams.

An account of the hoax contained in the September 16, 1897, issue of the *Sandy Creek News*, states that the incident occurred "many years ago," so this would probably place the happening back in the 'sixties or 'seventies.

Mr. Hull, in a newspaper account accompanied by a carefully prepared scientific explanation, declared the heavenly visitor to be the "size of a haystack above ground," and probably twice that bulk buried in the soil. Soon newsmen from far and near, as well as scientists from several universities, began to arrive in Oswego on the trail of the meteor. All were directed to visit Mr. Hull, the authority on the subject, who was enjoying himself immensely.

No, he had not seen the meteor himself, being too busy and not much interested in meteors anyway. His only knowledge of the affair was what had been told him by a farmer who lived in the vicinity and had seen the meteor fall. That queer looking black stuff on his desk? Yes, that was a chunk that had been knocked off the meteor by the farmer, who had visited the place next day. No, he didn't care to part with it, but he would, reluctantly, in the interest of science.

He would then bow the exultant interviewer out, supposedly in possession of the only sample of the meteor available, and then go back to his desk, reach into a box underneath and take out another piece of slag, which he would place upon the desk in readiness for the next visitor.

Excited searchers would hire conveyances and drive the many miles to the supposed location of the scientific wonder, and after searching diligently, sometimes for days, would have to give up in despair, This went on for a couple of weeks, and when nobody had reported any success, a few began to suspect that perhaps they had been duped. Finally several of them in a body visited Mr. Hull's office and told him bluntly that they thought there was a "skunk in the woodpile" somewhere.

Mr. Hull expressed great surprise that they had not located the meteor, saying that the Boyston hills were a wild and wooly area, and that they might have missed it by only a few feet. But when told that there was nothing to be surprised at, as there had never been a meteor fall in the area, he admitted ruefully that he might have been the innocent butt of a practical joke, and he expressed great sorrow that anyone would lie as his informant must have done.

There were quite a few angry words and some threats uttered, but they all rolled off Mr. Hull like water off a duck's back, and soon the "shouting and the tumult died," and the reporters and the scientists departed for their respective starting points.

And this was all the satisfaction that they derived from all their trouble.

THE SALMON RIVER POET

Sam Hardy, later known as "The Poet of Salmon River," was born in the early 1850's, and was brought to Montague as a small boy when his father, Sam Hardy, Sr., came to the area in 1858. With the elder Mr. Hardy also came Jerome B. Greenfield and George Bowman, to become the earliest settlers in the Town of Montague.

These men had fond hopes of establishing large and prosperous farms on the banks of the north branch of Salmon River (Mad River) and the vicinity where they built their homes became known as "Salmon River," and was situated near where the settlement of Hooker later developed.

The hopes of profitable farming in the area came to naught, due to the short growing seasons, long winters with heavy snows, scarcity of roads, and isolation from markets. Farms and buildings were abandoned and disappeared, settlers moved away, and the region reverted to the wilderness.

But still the younger Sam Hardy continued to live in a small shack hidden in the evergreens near the banks of Mad River. His love of the region, of which he had come to know every nook and cranny, would not let him move away. Apparently somewhere along the way he must have taken a wife, as a yellowed newspaper clipping refers to the fact that, in his later years, he would sometimes journey to Lowville to visit his daughter for a few days. This, apparently, was his only contact with civilization except for the few hunters and trout fishermen who penetrated the dense forests surrounding his abode. His living was derived from hunting, fishing, trapping, and a limited type of farming, by which he raised enough vegetables to take care of his modest needs. His education was practically nill, being limited to writing his name in a somewhat illegible manner, and perhaps a recitation of the lower multiplication tables. But he was a very talented maker of rhymes, most of which he carried in his head, as he was incapable of putting them down in writing.

But sometimes when he was visiting Lowville, he would also visit his old friend, Frank Bowman, a noted barrister and one-time president of the Lewis County Bar Association, to whom he would recite his latest compositions. Mr. Bowman would transcribe them, and in this manner some of them were preserved. It is said of his creations that "they had a sort of Robert Service style, with here and there a Kiplingesque line thrown in."

His masterpiece, "The Ballad of Salmon River," is one of the few samples of his poetic ability still in existence. In it he displayed an almost polished sense of pentameter and rhythm that might well be emulated by present-day writers of "free verse," and must have been natural rather than acquired.

The "ballad" was prompted by a legal dispute brought on by a man named Dikes having bought a piece of land on which George Bowman and Jerome Greenfield held a life lease, of which Mr. Dikes knew nothing at the time of purchase. Being what was known in those days as a pettifogger, or unofficial lawyer (also referred to as "side-hill lawyer"), Mr. Dikes immediately set out to dislodge the two lessees from the land. Failing to do this by legal means, he one night attempted to drive away a herd of cattle pastured there, but was apprehended and very severely handled by the owners of the cattle; whereupon he had them arrested and charged with assault and battery. It was the outcome of this case that furnished the inspiration for Sam Hardy's ballad.

It will be noted that reference is made to one man who sided with Mr. Dikes in the controversy, who said that he would believe the man's word "as quick as Bible truth." It is further insinuated that Mr. Dikes stole a load of logs which he drew to this man's sawmill, where they were surreptitiously sawed into lumber by the mill owner. This was possibly the result of the partisanship that can occasionally arise in such neighborhood disputes. The possibility of its having been true were very small, as the allusion was to Ralph Hooker, a retired minister, who was owner of Hooker's Mill and founder of the settlement that bore his name. Mr. Hooker was known to have been a man of high integrity and unimpeachable character.

The Ballad seems to leave the outcome of the case rather hanging in mid-air, with Dikes in jail and consigned by the poet to stay there until Judgement Day . . . "Til Dikes goes down beneath John Brown, where he will need no wood." As wood was the universal Tug Hill fuel at that time, the poet couldn't have meant anything else but Hell.

Mr. Hardy died in 1936, and is buried in the Liberty cemetery, located northwest of Liberty on the "Liberty Road" to New Boston. This is the oldest of two cemeteries located in the Town of Montague, whose population has dropped from almost one thousand in 1880 to seventy-three in 1960.

THE BALLAD OF SALMON RIVER

In Montague (pronounced Mon-Tag-You) I
  own 'tis true,
With cold we often shiver.
But the chilliest blast has come at last,
Direct from Salmon River.

For Lawyer Dike has made a strike,
And traded off his farm.
For land away down in LeRay,
Where I hope he'll do no harm.

Although he took the contract o'er,
He says it will not stand.
Because he did not know before,
Of a life lease on the land.

The lawyer's got a suit commenced,
For fraud, I think he said,
Because he couldn't use the land,
'Til another man was dead.

But the fraud was on the other hand,
As circumstances show.
And Dike with speed, and hired steed,
Quickly to town did go.

The neighbors near the lawyer's farm,
Were drawn into the fight.
Having hired the farm for a term of years,
On assurance that all was right.

They were not afraid of his parade,
As actions spoke most sure;
For they cut the hay, and drew it away,
And also the manure.

Then Dike did find no drove of swine,
On which to edge the battle,
But soon he spies, with longing eyes,
A herd of grazing cattle.

And out he flies, and the lash applies,
And makes the cowbells rattle.
O'er stones and logs, and brush and bogs,
He rushes on the cattle.

202

The neighbors roused by lowing cows,
Rushed to the scene of action;
And Dike and kine, 'twas there, they find,
Cavort in rapid traction.

These men of strength became at length,
Quite vexed, there is no doubt.
And told him he must stop the chase,
Or else they'd cast him out.

Then Satan turns, with anger burns,
And leaves the cattle tails,
But soon he finds his neck combines,
Against the pasture rails.

He sore repents when on the fence,
But as soon as he is free,
He swears that he will take them for,
Assault and batter-ee.

Now, to conclude this brief prelude,
And make my story short;
He took them down to a nearby town,
And bound them o'er to Court.

There to appear, and if not clear,
I think they'll make him smart;
For he will find no neighbors near,
Who'll choose to take his part.

Stop, I forget; there is one yet,
An acquaintance from his youth,
Who says that he'd believe Dike's word,
As quick as Bible truth.

One woman frail, who did assail,
By swearing Dike stole logs.
This friend of his, on high heels riz,
And howled like the dogs.

And when poor Dike worked day and night,
These stolen logs to draw,
His faithful friend his time did spend,
These self-same logs to saw.

In jail Dike lies, with tearful eyes —
We pray that he may stay,
'Til angel "Gabe" his trumpet shall blow
Upon the Judgement Day.

Now let us strive, while we're alive,
To do each other good.
'Til Dike goes down, below John Brown,
Where he will need no wood.

Composed by Sam Hardy,
The Poet of Salmon River.

THE NORMAN CROSSETT
MYSTERY

A tragedy that posed a mystery which has never, to this day been solved, occurred in Oswego County in 1863, near the famous high falls on Salmon River.

It was on a balmy Sunday morning in early May that Norman Crossett, son of a farmer in the Orwell-Altmar area, set out with his twelve-year-old twin brother George on a trout-fishing trip into the nearby forest. Accompanying them was another boy named Charles Gurley, a few years older, and the son of the couple who owned and operated the well-known Cataract House at Salmon River Falls, a favorite hostelry for vacationers in those days.

The long-planned fishing trip, coupled with the beautiful spring day, was the source of a great deal of elation to the boys, and they were in high spirits as they plunged into what was then known as the Big Woods, a vast tract of almost pathless wilderness between Orwell and Redfield Square. But like most pioneer youths, the fact that these woods were virtually unexplored held no terrors for them.

They found the stream for which they were headed with no difficulty, and the fish being very cooperative, by afternoon they had all the trout that they cared to carry home. So for an hour or so they lolled on the stream bank, talking and playing tricks as boys will at such times.

By late afternoon they decided that it was time to start for home, and it was then that Norman, whom everyone called "Towhead," announced that he knew another and shorter route home, and that he intended to return that way. In vain his companions tried to dissuade him.

"It would be awful easy to get lost in these here woods," protested George, the twin brother. "You'd best come with us, Towhead."

But Towhead was obstinately set upon following the new way, and would not let anything change his mind.

"I'll beat you fellers home by half an hour," he called back as his companions watched him disappear into the dense forest. And that was the last that they, or any of his other friends or relatives, ever saw of Towhead Crossett.

George and Charles arrived home well before dark, to find that Norman had not as yet shown up. But even as darkness settled down and he was still missing, no one was unduly alarmed. The weather was warm, and the boy healthy and used to the woods. So what if he did have to spend a night in the woods? It would just mean a little discomfort, and perhaps hunger, for him. And surely he would put in an appearance in the morning.

But morning came and still no Towhead. Noon rolled around and still no sign of him. By this time his parents were becoming slightly alarmed. As was the custom, guns were fired in an attempt to guide him home if he were lost. Word of his absence was sent out to the neighboring farmers, and a search was organized.

But that day passed, and another and another, and still no sign of the missing youth was discovered. As the news spread, more and more people joined in the effort, until it was estimated that at least a thousand searchers had participated in the hunt. Every nook and cranny of the woods for miles around was pried into, every stream searched, but no one ever discovered the slightest sign of the boy or his remains.

206

At last, after several weeks of fruitless search, the last of the searchers were forced to reluctantly give up. All but the father, who continued to roam the surrounding country in a vain quest, until winter and deep snows put an end to his efforts.

Many theories were advanced to explain the wierd disappearance. Some maintained that Towhead had been killed and eaten by wild animals, but at that date very few dangerous beasts remained in the area. And surely, if this had happened, there would have been scraps of clothing left as evidence. Some suspected that he had been kidnapped by a band of gypsies who were in the vicinity at that time. But certainly a strong and healthy twelve-year-old boy would have found some way to escape, or to get in touch with his parents. Others suggested that he might have fallen into some deep fissure in the rocks; but no such spot was known nor was any ever discovered. The possibility of his having been drowned and swept down some stream was investigated by thorough searches of all such possible streams from source to mouth.

The most plausible explanation to the mystery seemed to be that the disappearance was intentional and not accidental. Although no one had ever heard him mention such an idea, many who knew him suspected that Towhead, who was large and well developed for his age, might have slipped away to some recruiting center and enlisted in the Union forces under another name. Under the same name he might have been killed and buried; and thus his true identity would have been lost forever.

Whatever the answer, in more than a century the mystery has never been satisfactorily explained.

RUNNING GEORGE, BLACKSMITH EXTRAORDINARY

Almost every rural community possesses a character who, either by his eccentricities or some remarkable ability, or a combination of both, stands out from the multitude and becomes a legend in his own time. Such was the case of George Jackunski, variously known as Running George, George the Runner, and The Running Blacksmith.

Born in Pennsylvania, the son of Mr. and Mrs. Waclaw Jackunski, George was the second in a family of seventeen, and came to the Tug Hill area with his parents in 1914, at the age of twenty-two years. The family settled on a farm near Parkers, in the Town of Montague, and George entered the armed forces of the United States in 1917. His service in the 17th Infantry endured throughout the remainder of World War I, and having received an honorable discharge, he returned to his Tug Hill home.

George was a fine figure of a man. A full six feet in height, he tipped the scales at about two hundred and forty pounds. Not an ounce of this was surplus fat; all was solid bone and muscle. A total abstainer from the use of either alcohol or tobacco, he believed in the simple things in life: simple, substantial food to nourish his body, regular and temperate hours for rest and relaxation, plenty of hard work and exercise to keep himself in trim.

While going to school in Pennsylvania, George had

engaged some in athletics, especially in long distance running. In this sport he really excelled, and had won several medals attesting to his prowess in it. In later life he continued in the pursuit of this training, not as a sport but as an element of everyday life. If it were necessary for him to travel more than a few feet, it was always at a jog or full run. On longer journeys he might enlist the use of a bicycle, especially after reaching the later years of his life. After all, he maintained, that was "really only running sitting down." But on any journey of up to fifteen or twenty miles, it was always jog or run on his own two stout legs.

George's sister, who still lives in Lowville, commented on this:

"When we first came to this area,' she said, "people thought George was crazy because he did so much running. But he wasn't crazy. He merely loved to run, and I don't blame him. I used to love to run, myself, and did a lot of it. And I still would if I were a few years younger."

Very quickly George became a familiar sight as he traveled the dirt roads and trails around Parkers, Rector, Barnes Corners, and New Boston. And just as quickly he earned the nickname of "Running George," or "George the Runner." Some of the more unkind even called him "The Running Pollak," but this never bothered George, who was not ashamed of his Polish ancestry.

Somewhere along the line, probably while in the army, he had acquired skill as a blacksmith. He was especially adept in the shoeing of horses, probably because of his understanding and love of animals; and as horses were very abundant in the area at that time, his abilities were much called upon. Soon after returning home from the army he bought a small plot of land near Parkers, close to the banks of Edick Creek, and here he built a small shack in which he lived until the time of his death.

He became a regular employee of a blacksmith shop owned by Rex Sheldon at Rector, a couple of miles away.

But George's duties were not all confined to the shop. Sometimes a farmer miles away would want one or more teams shod, or a small logging outfit who could not afford to hire a full-time blacksmith would want some work done. Then he would travel the distance, always at a jog, with a pack on his back containing his tools, horseshoe nails, and a bundles of horseshoes that experience had taught him would suit his customer's needs. Some laughingly declared that he also carried his own anvil, but this of course was not so. Soon another nickname, that of "The Running Blacksmith," was added to the others.

The shack in which George lived was small and easy to heat in the savage Tug Hill winters, being only about a dozen feet square. Except for the packed earth it had no floor, and its roof was covered by strips of tar paper not nailed in place, but with the edges held down by flat stones and pieces of iron. A unique feature of this roof was its ridgepole, which was a steel I-beam rather than one made of wood. The rafters were made of heavy poles with the bark left on, and this combination constituted a very substantial roof that would withstand the weight of tremendous depths of snow.

The furniture that it contained came very near to being non-existent. A rusty cookstove served a double purpose as a culinary accessory and a heating agent. The only seat in the place consisted of upended blocks of wood, and an anvil mounted on another block of wood beside a ramshackle table.

"I never saw a bed in the place," George's younger brother, Wallace, told the author. "He had a big pile of old coats and blankets near the stove, on which he slept."

Contrary to what one would expect, George was an avaricious reader, and the humble abode was always well

211

stocked with papers, books and magazines. It was said that he "read everything from the almanac to the Bible." In later years he acquired a battery-powered radio that helped him to keep in touch with the outside world.

Fuel for his stove was brought from the nearby forest by hand-sled. In winter he used a pair of iron snowshoes which he had built himself, the weight of which would have bogged down an ordinary man helplessly into the snow.

Although he lived a simple and lowly life, George asspired to higher things. Throughout his life his one greatest desire was to fly; not by plane, but upon his own wings. Watching the birds flitting effortlessly through the air, he would envy them their ability and wish that he could emulate their actions. Upon several occasions he built himself heavy and cumbersome sets of wings that he fondly hoped would possess aerobatical qualities never before heard of. None of them ever worked, and George was always left with only his own two good legs as his chief method of locomotion.

Being primarily a fundamentalist, George loved all living and growing things. Several swarms of wild honey bees were captured and kept in hives near his shack, and he made pets of all the small wild animals living near him. No one ever knew him to needlessly take the life of a wild creature.

George was not without his human foibles, and one of these was his great pride in his prowess as a runner. One time at the Lewis County Fair in Lowville he was asked to make a running circuit of the race track. This he proceeded to do, not once but several times, and accompanied at first by a pack of admiring small boys. But these were soon left behind as George continued to circle the track, ever increasing his speed, and he was all alone when he concluded the run in a grand flourish before the

212

Old time Tug Hill woods crew. *(Photo courtesy Ethel Evans Markham)*

Relaxing on a Sunday afternoon. *(Photo courtesy Ethel Evans Markham)*

Inside the cook-house, the crew awaits dinner. *(Photo courtesy Ethel Evans Markham)*

This group of old-time lumberjacks found a new friend in this white-tail. *(Photo courtesy Ethel Evans Markham)*

Skidding and hauling horses on a Tug Hill logging job. *(Photo courtesy of Ethel Evans Markham)*

Loading logs at the log landing. *(Photo courtesy Ethel Evans Markham)*

Crew at landing between loads. *(Photo courtesy Ethel Evans Markham)*

A load of logs ready to go. *(Photo courtesy Ethel Evans Markham)*

It took a lot of skill and know-how to put a load of logs like this together.

Load of logs about to descend a hill. The men on the left will throw dirt under the sleigh runners to help brake the load.

Loading logs at the skidway.

Once more the woods crew relaxes
on a sunny Sunday afternoon.

The maple sugar house tank for
sap delivery in foreground.

Delivering sap to the maple sugar house.

All that remains of Running George's home.
Note flat stones on roof. *(Photo by author)*

The last steam roller in active road service
in New York State, with young operators.
Property of Town of Worth. *(Photo courtesy
Richard Knobloch)*

grandstand. After that, his run became a regular attraction at the fair for many years.

Running George lived in his little shack near Parkers for about fifty years. He let it be known that he had worked out a secret formula for staying young and thus warding off death. When asked about this formula, his brother Wallace made the statement:

"The only such plan that I ever heard of was his idea that constant running would keep him young and healthy. But old age and diabetes caught up with him just the same. He always had a horror of going to a doctor, and when one of his legs became badly infected, he still would not let one see him. That's what killed him."

Running George died in October of 1969. At least that is what the records say. But many of the residents and camp owners in the area where he used to run, and romanticists like myself, like to think that perhaps he is not entirely gone; that perhaps his spirit still jogs along the lonely dirt roads that he used to know, "sometimes running all night just for the sheer joy of running."

TUG HILL TRAGEDIES

"Happy events are soon forgotten, but a tragedy lives on forever." So said some long forgotten sage, and these words of wisdom, unlike their originator, have come down through the years to aptly portray an unexplainable quirk in human nature.

Somehow or other, a tragic happening captures and holds the morbid interest that seems to be dormant in every human being. Whereas a birth or a wedding are soon relegated to the half-remembered past, a murder or a death by accident are remembered for years; to be rehashed and discussed, and argued over and over again.

Perhaps this is a good thing. It may help to keep alive in the human psychological makeup certain instincts of self preservation that may assist in preventing more tragic occurrences.

However this may be, it is a fact that this fascination for the morbid was as alive in the Tug Hill region as in any other place. Because of it, many of the tragic happenings that have occurred there have been remembered, recorded, and brought down through the years.

Probably the vast maze of hills, gullies and swamps of Tug Hill witnessed many a tragedy among its early red-skinned denizens that went entirely unrecorded and unremembered. During the period stretching from the dim past up until the time when the inroads of white invasion forced the Indians to give up in despair, many a tragic incident took place. Certainly, since this was a favorite hunting and trapping ground of the Oneida branch of the Iroquois nation, there must have been

215

many times when an unfortunate encounter with one of the many savage beasts that then roamed the region led to death or terrible injuries to the hunter. And in addition, encounters with human intruders from the Canadian tribes to the north, or from the white settlements, must have led to death for one or the other.

Probably more tragedies would have occurred between red-men and white-men had it not been for the fact that during the American Revolution only the Oneida nation, of all the Iroquois tribes, remained neutral and friendly with both the British and the colonists. But, even so, probably many a forest encounter went entirely unnoticed and untold, its participants simply disappearing into the wilderness, never to be seen again.

Most of these incidents are lost in the limbo of forgotten things. Once in a blue moon one of them shyly emerges from the shadows and reveals itself to those who search for such things in the dusty corridors of the past.

*　　*　　*　　*　　*

Chief Poulus

One of these was recovered and related by John Clemons, historian, philosopher and jobber for the Gould Paper Company, who used to live in the Peekey neighborhood north of Osceola. It concerned an old Indian by the name of Poulus who lived near the spot where Swancott's Mills was later established. He was chief of a last remaining band of Oneidas who lingered in the area after the tribe had sold most of its land to New York State and been removed to a new location in the west. Chief Poulus, already an old man, begged to be allowed to spend his remaining years in the familiar surroundings of his youth, and he and a small band of followers were granted the request.

Even though old, Chief Poulus was a giant of a man

and quite famous as a wrestler. One day, at a pioneer rally near Potters' Corners, the chief with tonque probably rendered loose and careless by too much fire water, challenged any man present to wrestle him. The challenge was taken up by Gen. Pierepont White, who told the chief that he would wrestle him for all the land west of Fish Creek still owned by Poulus and his band. What the chief was to receive if he emerged victorious was not recorded.

The match was wrestled and Chief Poulus lost. Gen. White claimed the land, and the Indians were moved to a new site near Oneida. Only the chief refused to go. Moving far up Fish Creek, he built a shack and lived alone, running a trapline through the area to make a living.

One day in the fall of 1827 he went to tend his traps and did not return at night. The next day an acquaintance happened by, and noting that the old man had apparently not been home the night before, he set out along the trapline to discover, if he could, what had taken place.

Near the head of a small stream that ran into Fish Creek he found the old man dead, covered with blood and terribly clawed, and with a bloody hunting knife clutched in his hand. Across a log, facing him and also dead, lay a giant bear. Whatever had brought on the encounter no one ever knew, but each had inflicted the supreme penalty upon the other.

Leaving the two combatants as they were, the neighbor hurried on to spread the news. He also made all haste to get word of the tragedy to the members of the chief's clan at Oneida. Five members of the clan answered the summons, and refusing the guidance of the white man, they disappeared in the forest. Two days later they returned, but without the chiefs' body.

To all inquiries as to what had been done with the

body, they maintained a stoical silence. The next morning they were gone. And to this day, no one knows the last resting place of Chief Poulus.

* * * * *

The Coyle Mystery

In a section as wild and rugged as the Tug Hill Plateau, interspersed as it is by rocky ridges and summits, precipitous gulfs and gorges, and seemingly inpenetrable swamps and windfalls, it is not strange that so many people have become, and still do become, lost in it.

Usually these incidents have had happy conclusions, the victims having been either rescued by searchers or have found their own way out to some lumber camp or clearing. But there have been exceptions to this rule, wherein the victim was never seen again and his or her fate has remained a mystery to this day.

Notable among these was the case of Mrs. Thomas Coyle, a widow who lived alone in a house near the end of the Maple Ridge road, in the Highmarket area. Mrs. Coyle was in the habit of using a poorly marked forest trail to reach the home of relatives, the Kenealey family, who resided at what was then known as Number Six, later the terminus of the tram road built northward from Michigan Mills. This tramway had not at that time been built, and only the unbroken forest stretched for many miles to the south and west.

On Dec. 19, 1887, Mrs. Coyle made the trip as was her custom. After visiting for a while she started the return trip to her home late in the afternoon, and was never seen again.

The next day a neighbor woman who resided on the French Road, about a mile north of Mrs. Coyle's residence, sent her two young daughters cross-lots to carry some fresh-baked pastries to the widow, who was a good

218

friend of the family. Arriving at the house the girls found it empty. Furthermore, the fire in the stove had gone out, and the light snow that had fallen around the house the night before was undisturbed.

Hurrying home, the girls reported their findings, and an alarm was spread. A search party was immediately formed, and the hunt went on for several days, but Mrs. Coyle was never found. Neither was any track, clue, or indication as to her whereabouts.

Mrs. Kenealey, whose home she had been visiting, later recalled that about an hour after dark on that evening, she had heard a far-away sound in the woods, as of someone calling for help. Calling her husband, she also had him listen, but he dismissed the sound as the barking of a fox.

Conjecture as to what became of Mrs. Coyle has for years been a favorite topic of conversation in the farms and lumber camps of the region. Two years after her disappearance a skeleton was found near Michigan Mills and tentatively identified as that of the widow. But the identification was never made official, and the question remains: What became of Widow Coyle?

* * * * *

The Ingersoll Tragedy

Unrequited love has been the basis of many a tragedy, and such was the case in the death of a young girl of seventeen, a few miles northwest of Martinsburg in the year 1895.

This girl, a Miss Minnie Ingersoll, had become the object of an ardent infatuation by a man in his mid-thirties, whom we will refer to as John Jones. Because of the fact that he has relatives still living in the area who might be innocently embarrassed, his right name will not be used.

Although Miss Ingersoll had steadfastly discouraged the attentions of this man more than twice her own age, Jones refused to desist in his unwanted advances. As subsequent events proved, he had decided in his own warped thinking that if he could not have the object of his affections, then neither would anyone else.

On the evening of July 10, 1895, Minnie, a girl born and raised on a farm, was helping out with the barn chores on a farm owned by Jacob Strife on the Flat Rock Road, but leased and operated by her brother, Eugene Ingersoll. Mr. Ingersoll had been compelled to go to Lowville, a few miles away, and had left his young sister and an elderly hired man named Nicholas Strife to finish the milking.

Of course, the milking was all done by hand in those days. When a milk pail was filled, it was carried out through a long alleyway to an elevated platform. Here it was emptied through a strainer into large milk cans, in readiness for being loaded upon a wagon in the morning for delivery to a cheese factory.

Minnie had left the barn carrying two full pails of milk, and was passing through the alleyway, when suddenly there was a spurt of fire and the sound of a shot from an opening in a nearby box-stall. Struck in the breast by a heavy bullet, the young girl fell, milk flying in all directions from the pails that she carried and soon to mix with her life blood. She died almost instantly.

Startled by the sound of the shot, Nicholas Strife dashed out into the alleyway. Another shot rang out and he also fell, shot through the side. In the confusion that followed, a shadowy form fled through the open door and disappeared.

The cries of the wounded man soon brought help. While several neighbors attended Strife, another leaped astride a horse and galloped into Lowville to bring a doctor and alert the sheriff. Mr. Strife survived the shooting and lived to tell the story many times.

It took no great amount of sleuthing on the part of investigating officials to come up with a suspect in the murder. Jones' infatuation for Minine was well known, as was his apparent jealousy. Two spent .44 Winchester cartridges were picked up in the box-stall, and routine questioning the next day divulged the fact that Jones had, on the morning before, purchased a .44 Winchester rifle from Sterling's store in Lowville, along with ammunition to fit it.

It was later discovered that he had then hired a team and wagon and driven to the vicinity of Chimney Point Gulf, a short distance from the Strife farm, where he had concealed the rifle and ammunition in dense bushes. After returning the team and wagon, he had again gone to where he had concealed the gun, and fired a few shots to test its accuracy.

The present-day science of ballistics, whereby a certain rifle or revolver may be definitely proven to have fired a specific bullet, was in those days unknown. But the coincidence of the purchase of the rifle by Jones and the finding of the two expended cartridge shells of the same caliber at the scene of the shooting, convinced the sheriff that he was the guilty one. A warrant for his arrest was issued and the search for him began.

Although this search was diligently pursued, and the surrounding countryside scoured high and low, no trace of Jones was found until the following late fall, when he walked into the sheriff's office and gave himself up. It transpired that he had been hiding out in a series of caves near the head of Whetstone Gulf, a short distance behind the home of his sister. She and her family had supplied him with food, but she had also constantly urged him to surrender to the law, and it was due to this urging that he had done so.

It was later learned that this was not Jones' first venture into violence. In June of 1887, he had without provocation shot and wounded the mother of a girl to whom he was engaged, and had spent six years in Auburn Prison to atone for that crime.

At his trial he was found guilty of the murder of Minnie Ingersoll and sentenced to die by electrocution in the same prison during the month of February, 1896. The sentence was carried out.

* * * * *

Murder at Fowlerville

Fowlerville may be considered to have been a little removed from the Tug Hill watershed, being situated east of Black River in the southeast corner of Lewis County. But an event that took place there aroused the interest of the folks for miles around, and because of the excitement that it caused is included here.

On October 15, 1931, a young nineteen-year-old lumberjack by the name of Herschel Gardner, became embroiled in a quarrel with Clayton Thurlow, a somewhat older man. Whether or not liquor was involved in the affair it is now difficult to ascertain for sure. Possibly it was, just as it was responsible for many of the difficulties that arose among woodsmen.

The fact remains that Gardner, in a fit of ungovernable rage, seized a razor-sharp axe and hurled it at Furlow. The latter dodged the hurtling weapon,, which passed through the window of a nearby house, almost hitting an infant in its crib. Following this attack, Gardner knocked Furlow to the ground, and while holding him there, he slipped off his own wide belt, looped it around his victims' throat, and proceeded to choke Furlow to death.

Suddenly regaining his normal senses and perceiving

222

what he had done, Gardner fled the scene, not even pausing to remove his belt from about the victim's neck. Plunging into the Moose River, he swam across and disappeared into the dense forest.

Arriving on the scene, authorities quickly identified the belt as belonging to Gardner, and a wide search for him was organized. The next day he was discovered hidding in an abandoned house near the river, and he surrendered without resistance, after which he was lodged in the county jail.

At his trial, the charge of first degree murder against him was reduced to murder second degree, doubtless by virtue of the fact that he was engaged in a fight when the fatality occurred. He was found guilty and sentenced to from twenty years to life in Auburn State Prison.

* * * * *

Glenfield and Western Fatality

In the twenty-odd years of its operation, it is believed that only one fatality could be chalked up against the Glenfield and Western Railroad, and that was to a passenger, not an employee.

On the morning of August 23, 1917, Edward Darling, who was working as a cook in a lumbercamp run by Charles Ward, said goodbye to his wife and boarded a down-bound train for Glenfield. Mr. Darling was twenty-five years old and was heading out to enroll for service in Uncle Sam's army.

Everything went well until the train reached Bardo's Crossing, near Houseville. At that point something went wrong and the caboose and two carloads of logs were derailed. The caboose, in which the passengers were riding, was badly smashed by the tumbling logs, and Mr. Darling was trapped therein and crushed to death. Three other passengers were injured in the wreck, none seri-

223

ously. But Fate had decreed that Ed Darling would never serve his country in uniform.

* * * * *

Tragedy at Yerdon's Mill

Powered machinery is always dangerous, and with the abundance of sawmills on and around Tug Hill in days gone by, it is not strange that there were so many accidents, many of them fatal, concerned with their operation. One of these occurred on the morning of October 29, 1929, at the mill owned by Bern Yerdon on the Old State Road, a few miles north of Redfield Square.

Mr. Yerdon's mill, once very active, had at this time been retired to the status of custom sawing. Whenever sufficient logs had been accumulated at the mill yard to make it worthwhile, the mill was put in operation and run for a few days, or until the stock of logs had been sawed up. However, it had not been run for several months prior to the day in question.

On the day before, Mr. Yerdon had announced his intention of starting the mill, and had sent his grandson, Sterling Yerdon, who was then a boy of about eighteen, to contact Charles Barber and inquire if he could come and fire the boiler. Mr. Barber was an old woodsman and millhand, who usually did the firing of the steampowered mill whenever it was run.

In answer to the query, he made a remark which he had probably made many times before; but which on this occasion was clearly remembered because of its portentious nature.

"Yessir, I'll be there bright and early," he promised, "and I'll fire her or blow her sky high."

True to his word, Mr. Barber was at the mill with a fire in the boiler at six o'clock. The fuel for firing was dry, and soon the pressure gauge had risen to indicate a fine head of steam.

At eight o'clock Mr. Yerdon and Charles Caster, who was to act as tail-sawyer, were upstairs above the boiler room oiling the carriage, while Mr. Barber and Sterling were in the engine compartment oiling the line shaft. Suddenly, and without any previous warning of danger, the boiler room was filled with steam and a loud hissing sound, and the young man gazed upward to note that the whole front part of the mill had disappeared. Only the blue heavens above greeted his upward glance. But way down toward Cottrell Creek to the south, almost a quarter of a mile away, a hurtling mass of steam caught his attention. This was the body of the boiler, scattering steam, cinders and boiler fixtures as it went. As he watched, it struck the soft soil of the creek flats, tore an immense crater, and went careening on to half bury itself some rods further on.

Mr. Yerdon and Caster were upstairs, but fortunately not in the path of the hurtling projectile as it arced upward. They immediately scrambled downstairs, calling to find out what had happened, and who if anyone was hurt. Young Sterling answered them in a somewhat dazed condition, but otherwise uninjured.

"Where's Charlie?" queried Mr. Yerdon.

"I don't know," answered Sterling. "He was right here when she blew."

When the smoke and steam had cleared away somewhat, they found Mr. Barber only a few feet away, lying among the chips and sawdust. Carrying him out, they found that the top of his head had been blown completely off. Also, the soles of his heavy lumberman's shoes had been peeled cleanly from the uppers. Whether this was from concussion or some other agency, nobody ever knew. The hat that he had been wearing was never found.

Aside from a general shaking up and the trauma of horror caused by the tragedy, no one else was injured. But one curious fact emerged to puzzle the survivors.

When Herman Pratt, the attendant mortician, took Mr. Barbers' watch from his pocket, it was still ticking merrily away. But the watch in young Sterling's pocket, of a more expensive make, had stopped at exactly 8:03, the exact moment of the explosion. Upon examination it was found that the works were completely shattered.

"I sold it for a dollar, the value of the case," Sterling Yerdon told the author in a recent conversation.

Jut what caused the holocaust no one ever knew. Immediately after the tragic event, boiler inspectors conducted an investigation that disclosed that the boiler had been condemned as unsafe four years before. However, it had been repaired and used dozens of times after that, but in spite of several requests, no one had ever come to reinspect it. The safety valve was discovered and tested, and was found to have been operating at a safe pressure.

Mr. Barber was known to be a conscientious fireman who believed in always carrying the limit of steam pressure, or a little more. It was suspected that, like Jim Bludsoe of "Prairie Belle" fame, he might have "hung a nigger-squat (weight) on her safety valve." But this is only conjecture, and no one will ever know for sure.

* * * * *

Death in the Page Mill

Two other sawmill fatalities took place in the now long-defunct lumbering village of Page. Both illustrate very clearly how death constantly stalked the footsteps of the men who were engaged in this dangerous profession.

The first occurred on May 14, 1903, while a skeleton crew was readying the mill for the start of the season's sawing. Thomas Cunningham was crouched in the pit that contained the cable drum, making adjustments on the action of the carriage. This pit was located between

226

the rails on which ran the carriage, that part of the mill that carried the logs to and fro over the big saw. The action of this carriage was controlled by a lever in the hand of the head sawyer, who in this case was holding the carriage in place by a steady pressure on the lever. This, of course, was a dangerous procedure, to say the least. With a man helpless in the shallow pit over which the carriage had to pass, the power should have been shut off and the line dead, instead of live and potentially deadly as it was.

But no one knows exactly what happened. Perhaps the control lever itself was maladjusted, or maybe the sawyer just got careless. Anyway, the lever suddenly dropped forward from his hand and the heavy carriage leaped ahead and bore down upon the luckless Cunningham. There was not even time for a shouted warning before it struck him and crushed him against a bulkhead that formed one side of the pit.

The unfortunate man died almost instantly, a victim of unpardonable carelessness around sawmill machinery.

The second fatal accident in the Page mill took place a little over a year later, on May 25, 1904. In this case, also, adjustments were being made with full power on the line, a practice which seems to have been almost universal then, but which would not be tolerated today.

Alexander Dunn, a millwright, had been adjusting the tighteners on a thirty-inch-wide belt which ran from the steam-powered engine to turn a fourteen-inch pulley. This pulley in turn activated a line-shaft from which ran belts to various machines in the mill above.

As he turned to leave, Mr. Dunn apparently slipped and fell upon the swifty moving belt, and was passed two or three times around the pulleys before the power could be shut off and the machinery stopped. Of course, he was instantly crushed. One man who helped remove the remains from the belt, said that "he looked like a bloody maple leaf."

Mr. Dunn left a widow and family of small children, whom the demon of tragedy seemed to still pursue. During the following November, Mrs. Dunn left the house for a few minutes, only to return and find a four-year-old daughter, Ruth, burned to death. How the fire started no one ever knew.

*   *   *   *   *

Death in a Cloudburst

The afternoon of August 31, 1941, was typical thunder storm weather over the Tug Hill area. Unseasonably hot and sultry, the still and breathless air and towering thunder-heads presaged the violence to come.

Early in the evening the storm broke. Blinding lightning, accompanied by tornadic winds and rain of cloudburst proportions suddenly enveloped the entire region. Little streams that had been almost dry, fed by abundant water rushing down from the flanks of Tug Hill, became in moments rushing torrents that carried everything before them.

This included the bridge where the West Road, near West Lowville, crossed Silver Mine Creek, usually a small and placid stream. When the debris-laden wall of water hit the bridge, it was carried three hundred feet downstream, where it finally hung fast. The scene was now set for tragedy.

About nine o'clock that evening a car containing Bruce Robbins, his wife Ethel, and their five children, ranging in age from two to five years, was proceeding slowly along the West Road through the blinding rain. Also in the car were a friend, Maurice Fletcher, and a cousin, Stanley Robbins, who was the driver.

Suddenly, without any premonition of danger, the car plunged into the raging torrent where the bridge should have been. Immediately it was swept downstream

228

with its human cargo, finally coming to rest against the wreckage of the bridge.

Fletcher escaped through a window and pulled two of the Robbins boys, Bruce, Jr., 10, and William, 4, to safety by clinging to the bridge framework. Here he held them for over an hour, until rescuers arrived. Bruce Robbins, Sr., escaped from the car after it had been swept farther downstream, and made his way to safety. All of the other occupants of the car were lost.

A rescue party was quickly organized and began a search along the banks of the stream. The empty vehicle was found some distance downstream, but it was not until the next morning that the first body was found. This was of Stanley Robbins, found lodged against a tree in the deep gulf through which Mill Creek, into which Silver Mine Creek emptied, made its way through the village of Lowville. This was over two miles from the point where the car had first entered the water.

A little later, the body of Mrs. Robbins was found in the same gulf, and later still, the bodies of June, 7, and Richard, 2, were discovered near Church and Water Streets in Lowville. The body of three-year-old Janice was never recoverd.

Tug Hill is usually kind and benevolent. But this incident graphically illustrates the savage fury that the elements surrounding it can upon occasion inflict upon its people.

*   *   *   *   *

Three Men Die While on Way to Camp

Milford Widrick and Kenneth Lashaw, Lowville, and Bernard Grant of Potsdam started from Houseville to the camp of Kenneth Giffin Sunday evening, January 1, 1939, but were overtaken by a very bad wind and snow storm. The road led up the old Glenfield and Western tracks on Tug Hill, a well-known snow belt.

The snow increased to the point where further traveling became impossible. The young men tried to push the car from the drifts but, after several vain attempts, decided to spend the night in the car, with the motor running to furnish heat.

During the night the drifting snow completely covered the car so that the carbon monoxide gas had no way of escape except through the floor boards. The next day, the young men, covered with a blanket, were found dead in the car by Mr. Giffin.

TOLD WITH A
STRAIGHT FACE

As many an old-timer will remember, story telling used to be an art highly valued and much envied. It was a convenient source of entertainment at a period in history when, among the rural and backwoods dwellers, entertainment was at a premium. No television, no radio, no movies, back in those days, helped to pass away a few idle minutes; or to change the current of one's thoughts from the weighty problems of living to the lighter, brighter side of life.

So what did they do while waiting at the blacksmith shop for the team to be shod, or at the barber's when there was a long line of customers ahead; or at the crossroads store while waiting for the grocery list to be put up, and all the checker-boards were busy? They told stories.

Now these stories were not the risque type that one might imagine. True that some of them might be slightly off-color when the audience was wholly of the male gender. But usually they were of the tall tale variety, told solely for their humorous and entertainment qualities, neither believed nor meant to be. How these raconteurs could tell some of them with a straight face, with never a hint of a smile, is almost beyond understanding. But most of them did; in fact it was common knowledge that the straighter the face the better the story teller.

Here then (with a straight face) are some of the better ones that the author has heard down through the years.

231

Hunt Rowe used to tell a tale that was a dandy even for him, and as a teller of tall tales Hunt had no superior, and hardly an equal. It concerned an experience that had him really puzzled for a while.

"Was out huntin' one afternoon," Hunt would begin, with a doubt-me-if-you-dare expression on his face, "and my old hound started this big old buck snowshoe rabbit. I was standin' in the center of a roundish beaver meadow, with alders and brush all around it, and the danged rabbit started makin' the circle, stayin' just inside the brush. I shot at him three-four times — knew I was hittin' him, but each time I shot seemed like he run all the faster. Got so far ahead of the dog that you couldn't tell which was chasin' which.

"Well, sir, I seen that if I was goin' to git that rabbit I had to do somethin' different; so I slid over to the house, which was only a hoot an' a holler away, an' come back with my old 30-30. The next time that rabbit showed hisself I let him down for good.

"When I come to dress him out I found out what made him run so fast. A lot of them birdshot had got into his joints an' the cuss was runnin' on ball-bearin's. No wonder he could go so danged fast."

Hunt said that later he lost the old hound that he used that day. Seems that the dog had an unusual quality that led him to his downfall.

"Real smart, he was," Hunt would say. "Had him trained to hunt most anything. All I had to do was take a stretchin' board for the skin of any kinda animal I wanted an' set it outside the door. Danged if that old feller wouldn't go out an' bring in a hide to fit it.

"Well, one day the old woman had somethin' wrong with her ironin' board, an' she set it outside for me to fix. The old dog come along an' got a look at it, and with a kinda puzzled look on his face he turned around an' trotted off in the woods. We ain't seen him since."

232

Although most of his bear stories are true, Perc Caster can tell a tall tale with the best of them. Luckily, his friends can easily tell the tall ones from the true ones. One of the former concerns his boyhood in the environs of Redfield township, and the conditions prevailing at that time.

"Times was hard," asserted Perc, "but we always had enough to eat. Ma used to make buckwheat pancakes for breakfast, and what pancakes. Big as a kittle-cover and thick as a barn door. Only took a couple of them for a lumberjack breakfast.

"Winter come on about November and lasted until April, and I'll tell you boys, it really got cold sometimes. Old house we lived in didn't do much to keep out the winter breezes, an' the big kitchen stove couldn't begin to keep the place from freezin' up sometimes.

"Remember one time durin' a cold snap it got so bad that the only way we could keep warm was by fightin', mostly about who'd go outside and bring in the next armful of wood. Us boys was goin' at it hammer and tongs one mornin' when someone picked up one of ma's pancakes that had been left on the table and froze solid, threw it and hit my brother Clyde smack betwixt the eyes. Knocked him colder 'n a mackerel.

"Well, we dragged Clyde outdoors so's we'd have more room for fightin', and pretty soon the fresh air brought him to. He come back inside carryin' a big armful of wood, and that give us a chance to stoke up the fire and have a breathin' spell."

*   *   *   *   *

Charlie Hooker used to tell some dandies, especially about the years when he was "out West." Now no one knew for sure that Charlie had ever been any farther west than the shores of Lake Ontario, but he said he had been, so that made it so, especially for story-telling purposes. He read more Buffalo Bill and Young Wild West

233

dime novels than anybody else, so that made him quite an authority on the West.

"Wel sir," began Charlie, lighting his pipe and propping his feet up on the old pot-bellied stove, "rattlesnakes could be a real problem out on them prairies where I had my homestead. But I found a way to make good use of them. Yessir, I shore did.

"Ya see, out there trees are scarcer'n hen's teeth, an' it keeps a feller busy tryin' to scare up firewood. Lot of the time we had to burn cow an' buffalo chips, which ain't anything but dried-up dung. Burnt good, but was a little bit smelly. Yessir, a little bit smelly. But if ya wanted to burn wood, ya sometimes had to pack it for miles.

"Well, one day I was out hoein' in my corn patch an' I come across a big rattlesnake all coiled up betwixt the rows. Real mean, he was; yessir, real mean. I made a swipe at him with the hoe, aimin' to chop his head off, but I missed him an' he struck the hoe handle. Sunk them fangs right in, an' before he could get 'em out I'd stomped his head real good. Yessir, real good.

"Well, right away that hoe-handle started to swell from the pizen of that snake bite, an' it kept right on swellin' 'til it was most the size of a railroad tie. Plumb spiled the handle, but it set me to thinkin', an' after a while I got me a plan. Yessir, I got me a plan.

"First, I rigged me up a string loop on a pole, an' went out an' caught me about ten-twelve nice sassy rattlers, which I put in a big box. Then I took my ole pack mule an' went over to Dead Crick, about ten mile away, an' brought back a good load of willow whips 'bout the size of my finger. Took one of 'em and poked it into that box of rattlers, an' bang, one of 'em hit it. That there stick started to swell an' in no time at all it was big around as my leg. Yessir, size of my leg.

"Four-five trips out to Dead Crick an' I had plenty

234

of firewood to last all winter. But I also had myself a hell of a lot of work cuttin' it up, so I put on my thinkin' cap an' pretty soon I had me another plan. 'Stead of pokin' them sticks in full length, I started cuttin' 'em up to about a foot long. That way the wood come out stove length, an' done away with a lot of choppin'.

"Pretty soon I give up farmin' entirely an' just took care of my wood business. Hired on a couple of men to help me, an' sold to all the settlers for miles around. Was doin' real well until I'd used up about all the rattlesnakes in the country. Got so ya couldn't hardly find one. So when a feller come along an' made me an offer for the business, I sold out lock-stock-an' barrel an' come on back here. Yessir, I come on back home."

Many of Charlie's tall tales were about hunting and fishing experiences, and this is not strange when one considers the importance of these two activities in the lives of backwoods dwellers. Here is one that he liked to tell when his audience contained a few hunters.

"Now a coon is a good eatin' animal," he would begin. "If he's too thin to fry, he'll always bile. Trouble is, it usually takes two-three of 'em to make a meal, an' ya can't always find that many together. But I run onto a batch of 'em once that woulda made a meal for ole Paul Bunyan hisself. Yessir, I shore did.

"Was huntin' deer or most anythin' else that come along, up around Rimey Corners one day. Nice fall day, no snow. Got kinda tired an' thought I'd stand an' watch for a few minutes, so I leaned back up ag'in a big birch tree with a crack up the side of 'er.

"Well sir, all at once somethin' grabbed aholt of my huntin' shirt an' hung right on. I started to pull to git away an' pretty soon it let go. I turned around just in time to see the crack in that tree closin' up again, an' in about half a minit it started to open. Kept up that

235

open'n an' closin' about every half a minit. I'll tell ya, boys, it was plumb scary, yessir, plumb scary.

"It wa'n't too far out to the house, so I hustled out there an' come back with an axe an' crosscut saw. I knowed there was somethin' inside that tree, an' by cracky, I made up my mind to find out what it was. Took quite a while to git that ole tree down, but after a while she fell. There was a hole up near the top, an' coons started comin' out of it. Fast as one would show hisself I'd smash him over the head with the axe handle an' throw him on the heap. Pretty soon I had a pile that two tall men couldn't of shook hands over.

"Well sir, they kept on a comin', an' when that tree was cleaned out I started countin'. Seventy-six there was, not countin' a couple little half-growed titmens. An' then I knowed what made that ole tree act so funny. When them coons would breathe in, they'd spread that crack, an' when they'd breathe out it'd close up ag'in. Strangest thing ya ever seen. Yessir, it shore was."

*   *   *   *   *

The following humorous anecdote used to be told by the author's father, Ed Samson, who was in his day a great practical joker, and loved to tell a comical tale.

It concerned Rastus Clark and his son Arsey, who lived on top of Battle Hill near Loatwall's Corners, about halfway between Greenboro and Redfield Square. Rastus was a widower, and single-handed he brought up the boy, Arsey, who was a semi-cripple, having been born with club-feet. But there was nothing wrong with Arsey's other extremity; he turned out to be plenty smart in the head.

Ordinarily Rastus did his "trading" at Redfield Square, only four or five miles from home. But two or three times a year the wanderlust overtook him, and he would journey by horse and buggy to Lacona, a full fourteen miles away. Usually these sojourns began before

236

daylight, and the tail end of the return trip probably would be made by starlight. Rastus always took young Arsey with him on these trips, and this fact occasioned the tale which my dad used to tell.

"Well sir," he would relate concerning one of these treks, "when they got to The Crick (old-timer's name for Lacona) that boy's eyes was crossed and twisted something terrible to see. Nobody seemed to be able to figure out what ailed him, so Rastus took him in to see Doc Austin. It didn't take Doc long to diagnose the case.

" 'Rastus, how far is it up to your place?' asked Doc.

" 'Why, I reckon about fourteen mile,' said Rastus.

" 'Plain as the nose on your face what's happened,' says Doc. 'That young'n set there for fourteen mile and watched that front wheel go 'round and 'round. No wonder his eyes are all screwed out of shape.'

" 'But Doc,' says Rastus, 'what in tarnation am I gonna do about it?'

" 'Only one thing to do,' says Doc. 'Untwist 'em the same way they got twisted up in the first place.'

"Well sir, Rastus got that boy back into the buggy and backed all the way home. Arsey kept his eyes on that buggy wheel all the way, and although it took them longer than usual to make the trip, when they got home his eyes was all untwisted and back to normal again."

* * * * *

Another funny but probably untrue tale concerning this same father and son was also told. It seems that Arsey got the diphtheria one summer and for a long time hovered on the verge of death, but after a while he began to regain his health. When he was able to be up and around again it was just about haying time, and Rastus was hard-pressed for help.

"Now Arsey," he said to the boy, "you've had a nice long rest in that bed. Seems to me you'd aught to be able

237

to pick up that scythe and do a good day's work in the hay-lot."

* * * * *

"Sure, beavers are good workers," said Billy Ward Caster, squinting his eye thoughtfully at the group of lumberjacks gathered in the camp lobby. "They gotta be, else they'll git fired."

Knowing glances circulated among the group. A story was in the offing, they knew. Finally someone took the bull by the horns and asked the pertinent question.

"What do you mean by gittin' fired, Bill?"

"Well," answered Billy, propping his feet on the wood-box, "maybe it don't mean anything, an' then ag'in, maybe it does. All I know is what I seen with my two eyes."

"I'd been fishin' Beaver Crick an' was on my way home, takin' my time slow an' easy, when all at once I happened on a gang of beaver buildin' a dam.

"Now you understand, workin' beaver always keep a guard out to warn 'em in case any danger shows up, but this gang must've been short-handed, 'cause they'd kid-napped a couple woodchucks an' was makin' them do guard duty. Guess the woodchucks wa'nt none too fond of the job, 'cause they wa'nt payin' much attention to business. That's how I was able to git up so close to 'em.

"Well sir, I musta laid there for nigh onto an hour, hid in the brush an' watchin' 'em work. There was about twenty-twenty-five of 'em and they was all workin' like hell, all except one ole big fat feller that was actin' as boss. He was a-swimmin' around an' back an' forth, with a pencil behind his ear an' a checkbook in his paw. Bea-ver started layin' down on the job, the ole boss would swim right up to him, write him out a check, an' fire him on the spot. Seen him let three go whilst I was watchin', an' God only knows how many he fired after I left. Sure was a hard boss to work for."

238

Billy always had a good stock of stories on hand, and was always ready to tell one at the drop of the hat. One of his favorite shorter ones was as follows:

"Now you know the high falls on Mad River," says Bill. "Quite a little step off there — must be forty-fifty feet. Well, I was fishin' up above there one day. Water was just right an' the trout was sure bitin', an' I was so sot on fillin' my baskit that I got a little careless an' didn't pay 'tention to where I was goin'. First thing I knew the current took me right off my feet an' I was headed right smack for them falls.

"Well, I seen they wa'nt anythin' I could do about it, an' the trout was still bitin', so I just kept right on fishin'. Went over them falls slick as a whistle, an' caught three more trout on the way down. They just filled my baskit, so when I hit bottom I was ready to quit. An' I never broke a tail-feather on the way down."

* * * * *

A bunch of coon and fox hunters were swapping yarns around a stove in a country store somewhere on Tug Hill. As is usually the case, the talk and bragging turned to hunting dogs that each one had known or owned, and each story got to be a little wilder than the ones before. When the fertilizer on the floor had gotten to most boot-top height, one of the younger men spoke up.

"You can brag about your dogs of years ago," he said, "but I've got one right now that can run a fox trail twenty years old."

Immediately he was immersed with expressions of derision and disbelief. No dog could be that good, they all declared. Finally some one came up with the remark that he had five dollars that said the bragger couldn't prove it.

"You git your five dollars and I'll go git my dog," said the wonder dog's owner. Leaving the store, he was back in a few minutes with one of the sorriest looking mutts that any of them had ever seen. The dog really didn't look like he knew enough to come in out of the rain; but you can never tell.

Amid shouts of derisive laughter the crowd left the store and trooped up the hill to a spot where foxes were known to cross. Here the mutt was turned loose, and after nosing about for a bit, he let out a bawl and set off on what he announced to be a fox track.

After running a short distance he suddenly gave a big leap into the air, landed a few feet farther on, and kept right on going. All of the followers had puzzled expressions except one old-timer who had a knowing look in his eye.

Well, that dog went on for another quarter of a mile or so and then did the same thing again; jumped about six feet into the air and landed running. This time he really took off, howling at every jump, and soon left his followers far behind and ready to give up the chase.

"Dont appear to me as if that dog of yourn has proved anything," declared the man who had offered to bet the five-spot. "Seems to me you owe me about five dollars."

The dog's owner ruefully had to admit that he guessed his dog had let him down, and was just about to pay up when the old-timer with the knowing look in his eye spoke up.

"Reckon that dog was runnin' a twenty-year-old track alright," he declared. "Fact is, I know he was."

"How can you be so sure?" inquired the scoffer.

"Well," said the old timer, "twenty years ago there was a six-foot-high page wire fence in both places where that dog jumped."

*　　*　　*　　*　　*

A tale which somewhat strains the bounds of credulity used to be told by Mart Thorpe, an old-time woodsman who had worked in the woods in Michigan and

240

Minnesota, and so was considered somewhat of an uathority on "western" lore.

"Talk about wolves," he would say reminiscently, "now in Minnesoty they really had 'em. Big ones, too, nothin' like the little grey fox kind around here. Yes sir, them was real wolves—some of 'em as big as a horse, or at least a good sized pony.

" 'Member an experience I had with a pack of 'em onct. Ain't apt to forget it, seein' as how I had a real close squeak. Was workin' on a big log job 'way up in northern Minnesoty. One Sunday afternoon I borried the camp boss's horse and cutter an' drove over to visit some friends of mine in another camp eight-ten miles away. Well, we got to playin' cards an' chinnin', an' the next thing I knowed it was after dark an' I knowed I'd best be startin' for home.

"Hadnt' gone more'n a mile or two when I heard this pack of wolves comin' hard on my track and howlin' like all get out. The ole horse heard 'em too an' took off like all hell was after him, but 'twan't very long before I could see 'em in the starlight, comin' up real fast.

"Course I had a rifle in the cutter; no one ever traveled much without one in them days. Well sir, I started shootin', tryin' to pick off the leaders. Didn't have very many shells, so I had to make every shot count. An' I done real good too, never missed a shot.

"Fast as I'd knock one down, the other ones'd jump on him an' eat him up quicker'n scat, an' I'd gain a little ground. But pretty soon they'd be right back snappin' at the cutter, an' I'd knock over another, an' the same thing'd happen again. 'Twould've turned out alright if my ca'tridges had of held out.

"After I'd fired my last shot there was still one wolf left, the biggest one of the pack. An' he was still hungry, even after eatin' the last one I'd knocked over an' all the

241

ones before that. He kept gainin' and first thing I knowed he give a big leap an' landed right on the old horse's back an' started chewin'."

About here Mart would pause and close his eyes as though the story was ended. Soon someone would get impatient and ask the inevitable question, " What happened then?"

"Well sir,' 'the old fellow would resume, "you ain't goin' to believe this — but that wolf et himself right into that harness an' I drove him two mile back to camp."

*   *   *   *   *

Bill Stedman was an old guide and woodsman who lived all his life in the Redfield-Osceola area. Bill could, and very often did, tell a tall tale for purely entertainment purposes, and usually his stories were second to none. He especially liked to tell about the deep snows and the intense cold snaps that often visited the crest of Tug Hill.

"Remember one winter," Bill would say, "I was livin' in a camp up on Six-Mile Creek. Doin' a little trappin' an' a little huntin' when the weather wa'nt too bad. One night it come off real snappish like. Didn't have no thermometer, but if I did had it woulda been beggin' to come in outa the cold. I could hear the hardwoods poppin' from the cold just like rifle shots all night long.

"Next mornin' it was too danged cold to get outdoors, so I hung around inside the camp kinda slickin' the place up. Had'nt washed no dishes for a spell so I thinks to myself it'd be a good time to do it. I put a kittle of water on the stove to heat, an' first thing I knowed it was b'ilin'. Too hot for dishwater, so thought to myself I'd set it outside an' let it cool a little.

"Well, I opened the door, but before I could set that kittle down outside, that b'ilin' water had froze clean through. Fact is, it froze so danged fast that the ice was

242

still warm on the bottom side. I'll tell you, boys, it was quite cold that day."

* * * * *

And so, with face still straight (but slightly red), we desist from further contention with Baron Munchausen.

ABOUT THE AUTHOR

Harold Samson was born in the Town of Boylston in the spring of 1908, but at the age of two his parents moved to a farm in North Redfield, where he was brought up. This was only about one-half mile from the settlement of Greensborough, and both locations were well up on the western slope of Tug Hill.

His formal education was all acquired in a country school near where he lived. He left school at fifteen to work in the lumber woods and sawmills. All subsequent educahas come from voluminous reading and self-study. He has since worked as a railroader, factory worker, fabric cutter, journeyman carpenter and carpenter foreman, and now is employed as Bridge Repair Supervisor for the New York State Department of Transportation.

He served in the United States Army from May 1943 to February 1946, during World War II.

He has always been very interested in outdoor sports such as hunting, fishing, trapping, target shooting, etc. His hobbies include photography, gardening, gun and book collecting, and he has a large collection of Adirondack and northern New York historical literature.

He was married in 1931 and has two daughters, three granddaughters, and two grandsons.

His wife and he now have a camp on the banks of Mad River, where they spend considerable time in the summer.